ADMINISTRATION

Val Wa

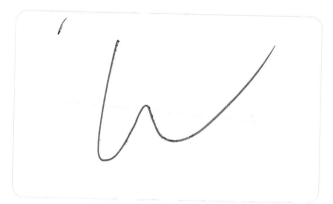

SO

NVQ
level

This boo

Student Handbook

Heinemann Educational Publishers
Halley Court, Jordan Hill, Oxford OX2 8EJ
a division of Reed Educational & Professional Publishing Ltd

OXFORD   MELBOURNE   AUCKLAND
JOHANNESBURG   BLANTYRE   GABORONE
IBADAN   PORTSMOUTH (NH) USA   CHICAGO

00 01 02

10 9 8 7

A catalogue record for this book is available
from the British Library on request.

ISBN 0435 45126 X

Designed by Ken Vail Graphic Design, Cambridge

Printed and bound by The Bath Press, Bath, England

Contents

Acknowledgements

The author would like to acknowledge both Margaret Berriman for her advice and encouragement and Sheri Hill for the professional efficiency and support which together greatly assisted in the writing of this book.

Especial thanks to Justine whose assistance in obtaining information proved invaluable. Her willingness to read through draft manuscripts and give opinions was much appreciated – however late the hour!

Introduction

This book is primarily aimed at students who wish to acquire a basic knowledge of office procedure.

All the underpinning knowledge needed for the 1994 NVQ Level 1 standards is covered in language which the beginner will find clear to understand.

The book is highly illustrated and office style activities throughout each unit offer ideal preparation for the Level 1 award.

The order of the units follows the NVQ Level 1 standards with additional units. Improving your Writing Skills, Applying for a Job and Interviews which the author considers students will find useful.

To maintain interest and to test and build on students' knowledge, each unit ends with a section review and either a crossword or word search.

Answers to all the activities and section reviews are given at the end of the book to enable students to check their own progress.

Contribute to the efficiency of the work flow

1

1.1 Organise own work

This section covers

▶ your own work role and responsibilities
▶ working methods
▶ managing your time
▶ working as a member of a team
▶ sequencing of work
▶ minimising wastage of materials
▶ working safely.

Your own work role and responsibilities

When you begin a new job, your employer *must* give you a **contract of employment** within thirteen weeks of starting work. One of the details set out in this contract should be your **job title**. Although not obliged to do so, many employers may also include a **job description**.

During your **induction** into the new job, your supervisor, or **line manager** (the person to whom you are immediately answerable), will generally introduce you to the people with whom you will be working and also inform you of the duties which you will be expected to carry out. Any instruction or training required for carrying out your work role should be given (or arranged) and any particular tasks for which you will be responsible should be explained clearly to you throughout this period.

Make a list of the duties which you carry out each week in your job.
Include any particular tasks for which you have responsibility.

If you had difficulty identifying your duties, perhaps now may be an ideal time to discuss your work load with your line manager so that your work role can be more clearly defined.

'At my previous work place, Mrs Pearson, we always did it this way.'

Working methods

As a new employee, you will not be popular if you make the mistake of telling new colleagues how much better things were done at your previous place of work. When moving to a different place of employment, the wise employee will learn to **adapt** to the working methods of the new job. This means following guidelines on how to answer the telephone, deal with visitors, document layout and even abiding by the rules on dress. Very often, these methods have been chosen by the management of the company, as the most suitable for the needs of their particular business.

It is essential that all employees follow the working methods laid down to ensure that

- maximum efficiency is maintained
- completed work is of the highest standard
- safety guidelines are followed at all times.

Many jobs involve maintaining records in relation to

- receipts and issues of stock items
- petty cash payments
- customer records
- incoming and outgoing mail
- receiving and making telephone calls
- visitors.

These recording systems have been devised to make things operate more smoothly and make co-ordination between departments easier. If staff do not conform to the accepted working methods of the business, the result could be chaos.

Managing your time

'I haven't done a thing all day ...'

Have you ever said this at the end of a working day? Not too often, hopefully! What you really mean is that you have not achieved everything you set out to do.

At the beginning of each working day, you have a good idea of the many jobs which need to be done or, alternatively, your supervisor will brief you on the tasks you are to complete.

If you fail to complete your work, it is usually because

(**a**) you have wasted too much time
(**b**) you have been subjected to interruption
(**c**) vital equipment has broken down.

Copy the following table and list the reasons why the daily work load may not be completed. Three suggestions have already been given to you. How many more can you write down? Compare your list with those of the other members of your group.

Reasons for unfinished work		
(a) Time wasted because ...	1 2 3 4 5	*Late for work*
(b) Interrupted by ...	1 2 3 4 5	*Lengthy telephone enquiry from customer*
(c) Equipment problems ...	1 2 3 4 5	*Photocopier jammed*

Sometimes it is unavoidable that you fail to complete tasks, particularly if you are continually interrupted, or delayed by equipment breaking down. However, if your work load is continually disrupted, discuss the matter with your supervisor, who may be unaware of the problem and may be able to offer some constructive suggestions.

Working as a member of team

If you were a member of your local football or hockey team, what qualities might make you a more respected player?

- Planning and discussing tactics beforehand
- Encouraging your colleagues to achieve success
- Giving 100% effort all the time
- Not wanting to take all the credit
- Not putting the blame on others when things go wrong

These qualities are also important if you are to have a good working relationship with your colleagues.

To work as a successful member of a team means pulling your weight, producing accurate work, offering to help colleagues who are under pressure and sharing jobs where possible – including making the tea!

Problems can arise when individuals want to take all the credit for jobs done well, or they produce sloppy, inaccurate work. Gossiping about colleagues, continually being late for work and taking excessive sick leave can also affect good working relationships.

Sequencing of work

Each day at work, you will be expected to make decisions. Initially you will rely on your supervisor to tell you which tasks need to be carried out first but, eventually, you will take responsibility yourself for the order in which you decide to deal with jobs.

There are many ways of reminding yourself of tasks which have to be done, such as

- a note in the diary
- a card index
- a checklist
- a simple reminder note to yourself.

You must learn to listen carefully and follow instructions which colleagues may give you either verbally or written.

e.g.

Get Mark Simpson on the phone for me immediately.

150 copies (stapled) for 9.30 am today please.

Remind me about this tomorrow morning.

Can I have the files for Denby & Co Martin Bros LK Components to take with me to London this afternoon.

At the beginning of each day, quickly check through the jobs which need to be done, giving them priority according to urgency – make a list if this helps. Throughout the day, you can then slot in urgent jobs as and when they are given to you.

Assume that you have arrived at your workplace – an insurance office – just before 9 am. Your job involves general clerical duties, including some telephone work and dealing with occasional callers.

Look at the list of jobs below which are waiting for your attention. Write down the order in which you feel you should deal with these jobs.

1 Paul Shannon has given you 2 pages of figures to be checked by calculator. He wants them before 2pm today.

2 30 page document needs photocopying and binding – before the end of next week.

3 Filing away documents and copy letters from yesterday

4 Your manager, Simon Watson, wants two files for Paul Heaton who has an appointment with him at 10am today.

5 The photocopier broke down at 5.30 last night. The engineer needs to be called out by telephone – urgent!

6 A cheque is to be made out for £284.60 payable to James Pearson, who will collect it at 9.30 this morning. Mr Watson will sign the cheque.

7 Mr Watson has asked you to telephone Acorn Garage to inform them that he will be about half an hour late for his 11 am appointment this morning.

8 Buy new batteries for the spare calculator – they were needed two weeks ago!

9 Make out a cheque to pay the office gas bill at the end of the month.

10 Two letters want typing for Susan Patterson. She is leaving for London in one hour but has said you can sign the letters on her behalf before posting them.

11 Telephone the railway station for Mr Watson to find the train times to London and return for his visit on Friday of next

12 Telephone Mrs Pamela Kent with some quotation figures for which she telephoned yesterday. – before 9.30 am.

13 Three letters to be typed for Michael Kenyon. He will sign the letters before he leaves the office at noon.

14 Type the Assessor's Report for Michael Kenyon for next month's meeting.

A helpful tip: if you are given a job which is obviously going to take a long time – perhaps days – to complete, break it down into sections and complete the task portion by portion.

Minimising wastage of materials

Look in your waste paper basket at the end of a working day. Is it overflowing with waste paper? Could this be through carelessness in having to start documents over and over again?

The majority of businesses can cut down drastically on the amount of paper used each day.

Tips to follow

Stock items
- Do not order excessive amounts of stock.
- Keep the stock cupboard locked.
- Insist on written requisitions for stationery items.
- Store stock correctly e.g. away from heat or in a damp-free room.

Photocopying
- Do not take extra copies 'just in case'.
- Check that the previous user has not left the counter set for 100 copies.
- Take a test copy first before making multi copies.
- For A5 size, place two copies side by side on A4 then guillotine.
- Fan the paper when refilling the paper tray to prevent sticking.
- Do not use the copier for *personal* copying.

Telephone/fax
- Plan phone calls before making them by jotting down notes first.
- Be brief – do not talk for longer than necessary.
- Do not use the fax for lengthy, non-urgent documents which could go by second class mail.

Consumables
- Have a desk tidy handy to keep all paperclips, elastic bands, drawing pins and other small items to be used again.
- Re-use envelopes for internal mail by covering the previous address with a stick-on label.

Finally, switch off lights and machinery if they are not needed.

Note: It is usual to leave photocopiers switched on all day because of the warm-up time and many are now operated on an automatic time switch.

Working safely

All businesses must comply with the Health and Safety at Work Act 1974 and subsequent EU legislation 1993. However, employees must also take responsibility for ensuring that accidents do not occur.

*See section 2.1 for **safety legislation** and **safe working practices**.*

Fill in the gaps in the following sentences. Choose only *one* of the two words shown at the end of each sentence.

1 Your supervisor will give you instructions for carrying out your work _____. (**roll, role**)

2 _____ can be one of the reasons for not finishing your work. (**interruptions, interviews**)

3 Each day you will need to check which jobs should be given _____. (**importance, priority**)

4 To avoid wastage, do not take _____ copies 'just in case'. (**extra, enlarged**)

5 Every effort should be made to minimise _____ of materials. (**wastage, ordering**)

6 If photocopiers are on an automatic time switch, it is usual to leave them switched _____. (**off, on**)

7 The Health and Safety at Work Act _____. (**1993, 1974**)

8 The person to whom you are immediately answerable is called your _____ manager. (**line, work**)

9 The new employee should _____ to the working methods of the company. (**adapt, adopt**)

10 To be a successful member of a team, you should offer to help _____ who are obviously under pressure. (**visitors, colleagues**)

Wordsearch

Look at the grid shown below and find the following words.

DUTIES

SEQUENCING

GUIDELINES

INTERRUPTION

SUPERVISOR

PRIORITY

WASTAGE

SAFETY

METHODS

TASKS

Q	D	F	R	T	Y	D	U	S	L	E	S
I	N	T	E	R	R	U	P	T	I	O	N
C	S	E	Q	U	E	N	C	I	N	G	M
D	F	U	D	G	H	N	V	C	T	Q	I
Z	D	B	P	F	W	A	S	T	A	G	E
G	U	I	D	E	L	I	N	E	S	C	V
Z	T	H	U	J	R	R	V	D	K	W	S
V	I	K	H	F	R	V	S	W	S	B	M
N	E	F	G	H	J	E	I	C	B	K	P
R	S	A	F	E	T	Y	V	S	B	Y	R
X	V	F	W	U	M	E	T	H	O	D	S
X	P	R	I	O	R	I	T	Y	C	R	H

1.2 Develop self to improve performance

This section covers

▶ identifying training needs/training specialists
▶ organisational training procedures
▶ preparing your portfolio of evidence
▶ obtaining proof of evidence
▶ action plans.

Success in your career is, to a large extent, mainly dependent upon **your own** actions.

Whether you are about to embark on your career from school or you are retraining in a new vocational area, your success will be governed by the amount of effort which you are prepared to make.

Begin by assessing what qualities you have to offer a prospective employer and how they will help you achieve your vocational aims.

Look back at your school reports or think back to how you conducted yourself in your previous employment. Were you

● punctual
● a regular attender
● conscientious
● reliable
● accurate
● determined
● honest
● a popular member of the class (team)?

These are the qualities which an employer is hoping for in prospective employees.

If comments such as 'could try harder', 'needs to concentrate more', 'attendance – 74%' or 'punctuality – poor' seem familiar *now* is the time to re-assess your personal commitment.

Identifying training needs/training specialists

Think carefully about what you would really like to do. Be realistic!

● Do you like helping people?
● Can you see yourself working with computers?
● Do you think you could be successful at selling?
● Does the idea of working with animals appeal to you?
● Would you like to travel?
● Does working with figures interest you?
● Did you enjoy your typing classes at school?

Find out what training opportunities are available. Depending upon your age and situation, the following specialists should be able to give you constructive advice.

Still at school
(or recently left)
- ✦ teacher
- ✦ careers advisor
- ✦ college tutor
- ✦ Careers Office

Adult returner
- ✦ College Student Services
- ✦ Training and Enterprise Councils (TECs)
- ✦ Job Centre
- ✦ private training centres

Employee
- ✦ managing agents
- ✦ employer
- ✦ personnel officer
- ✦ line manager
- ✦ supervisor

Don't forget that parents, relations and friends can be sources which are sometimes overlooked.

Organisational training procedures

Your current qualifications will probably not be adequate to take you through the remainder of your working life.

Let us take Jean, aged 46, as an example. She left school at 16 and started work in the accounts office at a local manufacturing company 30 years ago.

Her duties were dealing with incoming telephone inquiries, filing, typing invoices and statements and other clerical duties. She was also taught how to calculate the wages and simple book-keeping procedures.

Jean is still with the same company but she has progressed and now holds the position of Administrative Officer and is responsible for supervising a staff of ten.

Compare how work systems have changed since the introduction of new office technology over the last 30 years.

Over the years, Jean's employers have arranged for her to attend numerous training courses to enable her to keep her skills up to date and to cope with new computerised systems which they have introduced to deal with the work load. She has also been encouraged to attend her local college to achieve more vocational and professional qualifications. Jean's training has included:

✔ Beginner's Typing Class	1 year day release
✔ Switchboard Instruction from BT	half day
✔ Associated Accounting Technician (Foundation)	1 year day release
✔ Associated Accounting Technician (Intermediate)	1 year evening course
✔ Associated Accounting Technician (Final)	1 year evening course
✔ National Examining Board of Supervisory Management (NEBSM)	1 year evening course
✔ Beginner's Word Processing	1 year evening course
✔ Introductory Course for Spreadsheets	2 days
✔ Introduction to Database	1 day residential
✔ Intermediate Word Processing	1 year evening course
✔ First Aider Course	2 days
✔ Intermediate Course for Spreadsheets	2 days
✔ Certificate in Supervisory Management	1 year evening course
✔ Fire Fighting Course	half day
✔ D32/33 NVQ Assessor Award	half day for 3 weeks.

Jean has also attended evening courses to acquire skills and knowledge for her own personal satisfaction in a variety of areas:

✔ Flower Arranging
✔ Aromatherapy
✔ Keep-Fit
✔ Golf
✔ Cordon Bleu Cookery
✔ Holiday French for Beginners
✔ Piano lessons.

If you want to make progress in your career, you must be prepared to take training opportunities when they are offered by your employer.

Visit you local college and find out what courses they offer, either vocational or for your own personal development. Discuss the possibility of further training with your line manager.

Remember that, in addition to attending external training courses, many companies arrange for on-the-job training, in-house courses, demonstrations of equipment on the premises and – of course – the National Vocational Qualifications framework enables you to achieve accreditation by demonstrating and proving competence whilst carrying out your day-to-day duties.

If you have not already got a copy, ask you supervisor for the NVQ level 1 *Schedule of Units and Elements for the Administration Diploma.*

Identify the areas of each element for which you feel you can claim accreditation through your performance at work. At your next appraisal with your line manager, you can then discuss the NVQ elements for which you need assistance or training in order to achieve competence.

Preparing your portfolio of evidence

As part of your course you will undertake a variety of tasks to prove that you are competent with certain office systems and types of equipment.

You will be recording evidence of the work you have done in your record or log book to show to your Verifier/Moderator, along with examples of work you have produced, neatly presented in a portfolio.

To prepare your portfolio – materials required

1   An A4 ringed binder (or lever arch file)

2   A list showing the units for the NVQ Level 1 Administration Diploma, together with a breakdown of the competence standards

3   A divider for each unit number (*not* element)

4   A piece of A4 stout card to prepare your title page

5   A punch

Using your file

1   Work you produce within *one* unit or element should be filed, with a copy of the activity instructions, behind the unit number to which it refers.

2   Work you produce which 'crosses over' *several* unit areas should be filed in the **main unit area**.
    Next enter the details of this task on *all* the cross-reference cards for the other areas covered.
    At the end of the course you can type up your cross-reference information neatly from the card.
    It is suggested that on the cross-reference card you use the following headings:
    Date   Task description   Unit work filed under

3   Examples of work you produce on work experience or at work can also be included.

4   If you produce work you cannot punch, this can be included in a transparent file pocket.

5   If you and your colleagues are involved in organising or helping at a special event you may wish to take photographs to show the Verifier/Moderator. Paste these on to a sheet of A4 paper and add a written description of the event and how you were involved.

Special notes

1   You may wish to personalise your portfolio with your name and course. Do this neatly in a businesslike way – do not include any drawings or sketches on the front!

2   Make sure all your papers are punched correctly. *Always* align the papers with the central mark on the punch to make sure they are 'square' inside your portfolio.

3   Keep your portfolio in a very safe place!

Setting up your file

1   Prepare your title page either using a stencil template or printing it out using desk top publishing, with the following details:

```
                      Your name




                PORTFOLIO OF EVIDENCE
                  FOR ADMINISTRATION
                     NVQ LEVEL 1










              Name of college/organisation
```

2   Label the **tab** of the unit *neatly* across the front of the divider.

3   File the relevant competence standards behind each unit divider for easy reference.

4   Print the **title** of the **unit list** at the front of your file to act as the index.

5   You could prepare an organisation chart of the company you work for showing your department, line manager and supervisor together with a brief job description of yourself. File this behind your title page.

6   Eventually, you can prepare a *curriculum vitae* (CV) to put behind the title page, which will give some details about yourself and your experience to date.

See page 158 for the layout of a CV.

Obtaining proof of evidence

The secret of compiling a good portfolio is – **be selective**! Follow these guidelines.

✔ Check that the example of your work covers the competence criteria exactly.

✔ Nine or ten examples of one competence are *not* usually necessary – unless this is a specific requirement. e.g. *'4 print-outs are required'*

✔ Choose only *perfect* work, neatly presented for inclusion in your portfolio.

✔ Mark each piece of evidence with the date on which it was carried out, and where. Briefly describe how you carried out the task if necessary.

e.g. *'January – June 199-*
Copies taken from Visitors' Register
at Ensign Manufacturing plc showing
visitors with whom I have dealt.'

✔ As your portfolio grows, you may decide to separate the **elements** within each **unit** with sheets of coloured A4 paper (not dividers) suitably labelled.

e.g. `Unit 8 – HANDLE MAIL`
`    ELEMENTS 8.1 Receive, sort and distribute mail`
`             8.2 Dispatch mail`

✔ If you have received an excellent reference from a work experience supervisor, file a copy behind your CV at the front of your file.
Other references could also be included from your school, college or a part-time job employer.
A composite picture of yourself is being built up to illustrate to the Verifier/Moderator the type of person you are.

✔ Letters from previous employers or work experience supervisors *must* cover the criteria fully

not   *'Sarah's duties included, telephone, filing and mail'.*

✔ If the letter covers several unit areas
either photocopy the letter and place a copy in each area, with the relevant paragraph marked with highlighter pen
or   cross-reference this evidence as explained on page 90, under 'Using your file'.

✔ Bulky evidence such as tapes, photographs, large posters or booklets must be clearly labelled with the element number to which it relates and can be
either placed in a transparent file pocket in your portfolio
or   kept in a separate wallet folder or small box, clearly labelled for easy reference.

Remember: 1 Your Assessor, Verifier/Moderator and *you* must be able to find any piece of evidence *quickly*.

2 The quality of your portfolio reflects what type of worker you are – what image do you want to convey?

Action plans

Let us return to the remark made in the opening paragraph of this section:

---

*'Success in your career is, to a large extent, mainly dependent upon **your own** actions.'*

You should now be aware of

- the qualities you can offer an employer
- the different types of training specialists available
- the need for regular training throughout your working life
- the importance of gathering evidence of competencies for your NVQ portfolio.

What next?

You would be wise to draw up an **action plan** setting out what you want to achieve and the most sensible route for doing this.

Write down the following headings:

What I want to achieve	Route to take	Realistic achievement date

In the first column ...

Jot down every objective you want to achieve. Suggested targets could be

- learn to type
- lose 10 lb (5 kg) in weight
- take a 10 week holiday language course for Spanish
- join a class for RSA 1 word processing
- resit GCSE maths
- save up for a second-hand car.

In the second column ...

State how you are going to achieve each objective.

In the third column ...

Put down a **realistic** achievement date.

Refer to this action plan regularly to remind yourself of the route you want to take. Revise it, if necessary and – most important of all – tick off those targets you manage to achieve.

Periodically, your work will be reviewed by your line manager or supervisor. These interviews are called **appraisals** and they give you the opportunity to discuss any problems or plans which you may have.

You could discuss your action plan at one of these appraisals and your line manager may offer constructive advice about achieving some of your targets.

The ultimate aim after all is that you move forward – not stand still.

SECTION REVIEW

Complete the sentences below, using each of the following words *once* only.

appraisal	portfolio
TEC	Job Centre
action plan	in-house
line manager	cross-reference
vocational	punctuality

1 Training courses can be either _____ or for your own personal development.

2 Your _____ is the person to whom you are immediately answerable.

3 Courses which are arranged by your employer on the company premises are known as _____ training.

4 Training advice could be obtained from your local _____ .

5 It is advisable to _____ evidence which covers more than one area.

6 The binder in which all your evidence is gathered is known as a _____ .

7 An _____ is a meeting with your line manager to discuss your progress.

8 _____ is what all employers are hoping for in prospective employees.

9 The adult returner will find vacancies for employment at the local _____.

10 Objectives which you would like to achieve in the future should be listed in your _____.

Wordsearch

Look at the grid shown below and find the following words.

PORTFOLIO

TRAINING

PROOF

TEC

EVIDENCE

APPRAISAL

ACTION

VERIFIER

VOCATIONAL

ELEMENT

Q	E	V	I	D	E	N	C	E	B	N	T
D	Q	Y	P	O	R	T	F	O	L	I	O
X	W	Q	A	B	N	M	Y	A	V	T	A
X	W	E	L	E	M	E	N	T	V	B	P
S	W	F	G	H	N	O	V	D	G	S	P
T	R	A	I	N	I	N	G	D	S	W	R
X	W	A	C	T	I	O	N	D	W	T	A
X	B	G	A	B	F	E	T	J	G	D	I
X	Q	C	B	O	F	E	S	W	A	J	S
V	O	N	O	F	R	T	F	L	P	D	A
V	E	R	I	F	I	E	R	F	J	M	L
B	P	F	D	C	W	C	B	G	H	J	Y

1.3 Maintain own work area to assist work flow

This section covers

▶ your work area
▶ assisting the work flow
▶ storing or disposing of items not currently required
▶ reporting procedures to maintain a safe working environment.

Your work area

It is impossible to produce good work if you operate in a muddle!

You are responsible for your own work area and others will be quick to notice how well organised you are – or otherwise.

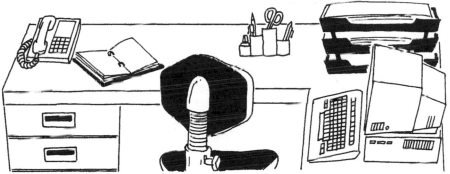

An ideal desk layout

Points to consider

- An L-shaped desk is ideal (a keyboard can be placed to one side).
- A swivel chair gives easy movement to a keyboard.
- The telephone should be positioned to the left (or right side if you are left-handed).
- The diary should be easily accessible from the telephone.
- A desk tidy is useful for pens, pencils and small consumable items.
- Filing trays should be stacked to keep work papers tidy.

Keep the remainder of your desk surface clear for your working area.

Assisting the work flow

If you are working as a member of a team, you have a responsibility to keep the work flowing. This means *prioritising* your work to ensure that colleagues are not kept waiting for you to complete essential tasks.

Points to consider

- Use your diary as a reminder system for important jobs.
- Make checklists and tick off jobs as they are completed.
- File daily (or more often) to ensure that up-to-date information is available.
- Ensure that incoming mail is distributed immediately.
- Keep to deadlines for dispatching mail.
- Proof-read all work carefully – repeating work takes time.
- Make sure that all equipment is properly maintained.

Storing or disposing of items not currently required

Books and materials which will probably be needed throughout the day should be stored out of sight but stay readily accessible. Telephone and fax directories, folders, reference books, consumables (such as correcting ribbons) and all personal items can be stored neatly in drawers.

Stationery items should be kept close to hand in a deep drawer – preferably in suspended file pockets.

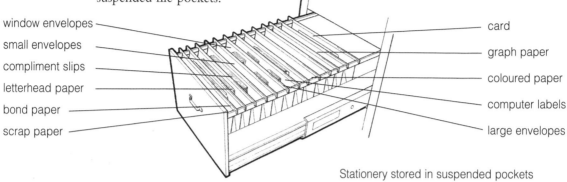

window envelopes
small envelopes
compliment slips
letterhead paper
bond paper
scrap paper

card
graph paper
coloured paper
computer labels
large envelopes

Stationery stored in suspended pockets

See page 136 for storage of stock. See page 86 for filing systems.

Reporting procedures to maintain a safe working environment

Why do accidents happen?

- failure to follow instructions
- faulty equipment
- inadequate training/supervision
- lack of concentration
- carelessness
- excessive speed
- untidiness

All organisations are obliged to conform to Government regulations relating to health and safety.

In your company, school or college there will be laid down reporting procedures in order to maintain a safe working environment for all employees.

See pages 19–20 for regulations under the **HASAWA 1974, RIDDOR 1985, COSHH 1989, Noise at Work Regulations 1989, Electricity at Work Regulations 1989** *and the* **EU Regulations 1993***.*

Employees must also help to maintain a safe working area by reporting

- damaged fire extinguishers
- all accidents which occur
- faulty equipment
- loose electric wiring and faulty plugs
- toxic chemical fumes.

In fact, any situation which could affect the safety of employees or cause damage to property should be reported immediately to a higher authority.

Fill in the missing letters and then write the completed words in your folder to help you remember what they mean.

1 To produce good work, you must keep your work _ _ea tidy.

2 The most suitable chair for an L-shaped desk is a _w_v_l.

3 A note in the diary will remind you of _m_ _r_ _ _t jobs.

4 Stationery is best kept in a drawer with s_ _p_ _d_d pockets.

5 All companies must conform to the health and safety _ _g_l_t_ _ _s.

6 If you are left-handed, the _ _l_ph_ _e should be placed at the right-hand side of the desk.

7 To ensure that up-to-date information is always available, you should file _ _ _ _y.

8 Reporting procedures must be followed to maintain a safe working _n_ _r_n_ _ _t.

9 To avoid having to _ _pea_ work, always proof-read carefully.

10 A desk _ _ _y is essential for keeping small, consumable items together.

Wordsearch

Look at the grid shown below and find the following words.

CHECKLIST

ACCESSIBLE

WORK FLOW

DRAWER

STATIONERY

TEAM

DESK

KEYBOARD

TRAYS

TELEPHONE

C	D	S	W	V	B	M	Y	O	L	E	W
H	A	C	C	E	S	S	I	B	L	E	B
E	F	B	G	T	Q	A	D	B	N	K	H
C	S	W	Y	U	D	R	A	W	F	R	L
K	W	D	F	G	A	C	R	P	U	T	I
L	Q	X	W	O	R	K	F	L	O	W	Z
I	B	G	B	Q	M	A	S	D	T	T	L
S	C	Y	N	A	D	T	U	Q	W	R	B
T	E	C	E	G	J	R	W	Q	N	A	X
K	S	T	A	T	I	O	N	E	R	Y	V
A	Q	Y	P	L	W	C	V	D	E	S	K
T	T	E	L	E	P	H	O	N	E	D	B

Contribute to the health, safety and security of the workplace

2.1 Contribute to the prevention of hazards in the workplace

This section covers

▶ recognising danger at work
▶ the law on health and safety (including EU legislation)
▶ safe working practices.

Recognising danger at work

Look at the pictures below. Each one illustrates *two* possible dangerous situations. Can you identify them?

Dangerous situations such as these are often referred to as **potential hazards**.

It is your duty to recognise potential hazards and, if you cannot deal with them yourself, you must report the danger to your supervisor or the person who has been appointed to look after safety matters in your building. This person is called the **safety representative**.

Make a list of any additional potential hazards which may occur in your school, college or workplace.

Compare your list with those of other members of your group and discuss with your tutor how these situations can be avoided.

The law on health and safety

In 1974, the Government passed the **Health and Safety at Work Act** (known as **HASAWA 1974**). This states that **both** employer and employee must accept responsibility for health and safety in the workplace.

The **employer** must provide

● a safe entrance and exit from work
● safe working conditions
● safe methods of operating machinery and equipment
● proper arrangements for handling, storing and using dangerous liquids and substances
● training and adequate supervision and instruction for all employees
● an enquiry into all accidents.

The **employee** must

● take reasonable care for his or her *own* health and safety
● take reasonable care for the health and safety of *other* people
● cooperate with the employer or any other person appointed to carry out duties under the Act.

Other relevant legislation includes

Reporting of Injuries, Diseases and Dangerous Occurrences Regulations 1985 (RIDDOR)

which states that all accidents and deaths caused by ill health at work must be recorded by the employer and reported to the enforcing authority.

Control of Substances Hazardous to Health (COSHH) Regulations 1989

which requires employers to

● eliminate or substitute hazardous substances
● control ventilation of such substances
● provide personal protective clothing for employees where control of substances is not possible.

Noise at Work Regulations 1989

which requires employers to

● assess noise hazards in the workplace

- reduce noise levels as far as possible
- keep employees informed of noise hazards and, if so requested by employees, to provide ear protectors.

Electricity at Work Regulations 1989

Organisations must inspect all electrical equipment on a regular basis to make sure that it is in safe working order (e.g. no frayed wires).

Look at the electrical appliances (e.g. computers, kettles, fires) in your organisation. Have they been checked recently?

If so, a small stick-on label will give the date of the last inspection. Make a note of these dates.

European Union Directives

On 1 January 1993, the government introduced the most radical changes to health and safety since the above 1974 Act, with the inclusion of six new sets of regulations stemming from European Union (EU) directives (called the 'six pack'). These are

Management of Health and Safety Regulations 1992

Employers are required to

- carry out risk assessments in order to decide what health and safety measures are needed
- make arrangements to plan, organise, control, maintain and review health and safety
- provide health and safety training to all employees.

Health and Safety (Display Screen Equipment) Regulations

This is the first set of UK regulations which provide minimum health and safety standards for the design and use of VDU stations.

Employers are required to

- make risk assessments of all workstations used by VDU operators
- plan the daily work of routine users so that VDU work is periodically interrupted by rest breaks or other types of work
- arrange and pay for VDU users (if they wish it) to have eye and eyesight tests, repeated at regular intervals and to provide spectacles or lenses which are necessary arising out of work with the VDU. (Employers are *not* required to pay for corrective spectacles for sight defects which pre-exist VDU use.)
- provide users with training about the safe use of their workstations and provide them with information to reduce risks to health.

Manual Handling Operations Regulations

- Employers must take appropriate steps so far as is reasonably practicable to reduce the risk of injury which could be caused to employees by the manual handling of loads.
- Employees must be told of any risks when handling loads and how best to avoid such risks.

Special note: *Never* attempt to lift objects which are too heavy.
The correct way to lift a load is to bend your knees and, keeping your back straight, lift the load so that the strain is taken in your legs, not your back.

Right way

Wrong way

Provision and Use of Work Equipment Regulations

Employers must ensure that

- equipment is suitable for the job it is intended for, and maintain that equipment
- appropriate training and information is given to employees
- any equipment provided after 1 January 1993 complies with the relevant EU directives.

Personal Protective Equipment at Work Regulations

Employers must

- provide employees with suitable personal protective equipment (PPE)
- maintain the PPE in good repair
- provide safe storage for PPE
- ensure that PPE is being used properly.

Note: To help prevent injuries such as repetitive strain injury (RSI), which is caused by making awkward repetitive wrist movements, protective articles are now available.

- 'Therapeutic gloves' – it is claimed – massage the hands during keyboard work, thus preventing strain. The natural hand heat within the Lycra glove produces a massaging and energising effect
- Wrist rests allow the VDU user to rest the wrists whilst operating the keyboard or mouse.

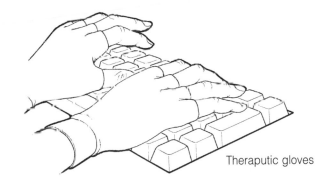

Theraputic gloves

Wrist rest for keyboard operations...   and the mouse

Workplace (Health, Safety and Welfare) Regulations

Employers must ensure that the workplace complies with the requirements set out in these regulations.

Health covering
- ventilation
- temperature
- lighting
- cleanliness and waste materials
- room dimensions and space
- workstations and seating.

Safety covering
- maintenance of workplace equipment
- devices and systems
- condition of floors
- falls or falling objects
- transparent surfaces
- windows and skylights
- doors and gates
- traffic routes
- escalators and moving walkways.

Welfare covering
- sanitary conveniences and washing facilities
- drinking water
- accommodation for clothing and changing facilities
- facilities for rest and to eat meals.

A booklet summarising these new regulations has been published by Labour Research Development Publications Ltd, 78 Blackfriars Road, London SE1 8HF.

Safe working practices

Employees should be encouraged to work safely.

Use of equipment *(See also Chapter 3, page 34)*

- Follow manufacturer's instructions.
- Check for trailing leads, broken sockets and frayed wires.
- Make sure that rings and trailing jewellery do not interfere with operating equipment.

- Arrange for proper ventilation when using equipment which gives off dangerous fumes e.g. photocopiers.
- Avoid leaving drawers of filing cabinets open.

Furniture

- Use adjustable chairs when operating keyboard equipment, to prevent backache.
- Use safety step ladders or safety stools when reaching for items from high shelves.

New technology

- Avoid operating VDU equipment for long periods without a break (can cause headaches and eyestrain).
- Eliminate glare on VDU screens by using sunblinds.
- Working surfaces should be at the correct height for either writing or keyboarding.

Good housekeeping

- Keep the working area tidy and clean.
- Store dangerous or flammable liquids and substances in a safe, well ventilated place in clearly labelled containers (**Note:** Thinners and ammonia need to be used in some copying processes).

Accommodation

- Offices can be closed or open plan. This means either a series of separate rooms or staff located in one large room separated by screens. Staff should not be overcrowded.
- Windows in direct sunlight should be fitted with blinds or curtains and there should be suitable lighting.
- Floor surfaces should be neither slippery nor worn.
- Toilets should be clean with hand-washing facilities.
- It is of benefit to staff if decorating is carried out on a regular basis.

Noise

- Keep to a minimum where possible e.g. special covers (known as **acoustic hoods**) can be placed on noisy printers.

Safe working habits

- Do not lift objects which are too heavy but, if unavoidable, bend knees, keeping back straight and take the strain in your legs – not your back.

Temperature

- Should be above 61°F (16°C) but not too hot.
- There should be adequate ventilation.

SECTION REVIEW

Fill in the missing letters and then write the completed words in your folder to help you remember what they mean.

1 The Health and Safety at Work Act 1974 is often referred to in the abbreviated form of H___WA.

2 Possible dangerous situations are referred to as p__ent___ __zard_.

3 Care should always be taken when operating __ch__ery.

4 In offices, the ___perat___ should be at least 61°F (16°C) after the first hour.

5 European Union legislation introduced in January 1993 is referred to as the 's__ p__k'.

6 When lifting heavy objects, the strain should be taken in your __g_, not your back.

7 Special covers, known as a___st_c hoods, can be placed on noisy printers.

8 Blinds will eliminate glare on _D_ screens.

9 The legislation governing the control of substances hazardous to health is known as C__H_.

10 Fire doors should always be kept _l_s_d.

Wordsearch

Look at the grid shown below and find the following words.

HAZARDS

ACCIDENT

SAFETY

RULES

AUTHORITY

DANGEROUS

ACT

POLICY

FIRE

ALARM

Y	F	S	S	J	V	H	B	K	G	S	W
S	T	L	U	S	W	T	C	P	U	T	N
L	N	I	O	P	O	L	I	C	Y	R	Q
O	E	F	R	A	L	A	R	M	S	U	M
J	D	B	E	O	E	V	K	D	D	L	V
X	I	N	G	K	H	S	F	I	R	E	P
H	C	W	N	Y	E	T	E	G	A	S	I
N	C	H	A	U	M	C	U	O	Z	T	M
Q	A	V	D	J	M	P	J	A	A	C	T
D	F	V	F	P	Q	A	L	U	H	L	C
F	W	G	C	M	O	Q	J	L	Q	Z	M
J	L	P	E	U	X	S	A	F	E	T	Y

2.2 Contribute to the limitation of damage to persons or property in the event of an accident or emergency

This section covers

▶ safety procedures to follow
▶ evacuation procedure
▶ fire fighting equipment
▶ accidents at work.

Safety procedures to follow

It is usual nowadays for all new employees to go through a period of **induction** when beginning a new job. This means being introduced to colleagues, the duties they will be expected to carry out, how the company operates (known as **working practices**), and familiarisation with the building and factory.

During the tour of the building, the new employee should be made aware of the following:

● layout of the building
● all entrances and exits (including emergency exits)
● location of fire alarms and how to operate these
● location and type of fire fighting equipment
  e.g. fire extinguishers
        fire blankets
        buckets of sand
● procedure for leaving (**evacuating**) the building in an emergency
● the assembly point
● method of checking that all employees and visitors have left the building.

> Can you think of any other reasons, apart from fire, why a building would have to be evacuated quickly?

Evacuation procedure

Fire is obviously the main reason for evacuating a building quickly.

Other reasons could be

● bomb threat
● toxic fumes
● risk of explosion
● gas leak
● flood
● power failure (plunging building into darkness).

During the induction period, all employees should be made aware of the evacuation procedure and shown where the nearest exit is.

Notices, outlining the evacuation procedure and giving the assembly point should be displayed throughout the building and all staff should familiarise themselves with these.

If you discover a fire

- Raise the alarm by using the manual fire alarm system or by reporting immediately to the telephone switchboard.
- Call for assistance and attack the fire with the fire-extinguishing equipment provided.

On hearing the alarm

- Leave the premises and report immediately to the assembly area, or
- Join the fire party if you are a member.

Do not stop to collect personal belongings unless it is obvious that there is a clear escape to the outside.

Instructions to the switchboard operator

Notice to be kept where the operator can refer to it instantly

- Call the brigade immediately by dialling 999 or the appropriate number.
- Notify a senior member of staff.
- Warn other departments and other offices in the building that fire has broken out.
- When instructed, sound the fire alarm or pass on the order to evacuate.

Do not

- panic
- use the lift
- re-enter the building until given permission to do so by the Safety Officer.

Fire fighting equipment

There are different types of fire extinguishers, each containing either water or a chemical suitable for dealing with a fire. Most fires fall into one of the following classes.

- **Class A:** wood, cloth, paper, plastics, coal etc.
- **Class B:** grease, fats, oil, paint, petrol etc.
- **Class C:** gases
- **Class D:** burning metals

To enable people to recognise which extinguisher to use for putting out different types of fire, extinguishers are made in various sizes and colours.

Fire blankets are made of special material and used for smothering flames e.g. chip pan fires. It is advisable to keep these blankets in a kitchen or other cooking area in case of fire.

Your tutor will give you a sheet illustrating seven different types of fire extinguisher (page 188). Note which extinguishers should be used to put out the different types of fire.

Look around your school, college or workplace (or other public building) and see if you can recognise any of these extinguishers.

Discuss with your tutor the different colours used for these extinguishers, then colour in the illustrations on the sheet with the correct colour. Keep this sheet in your folder for reference.

Note: All fire extinguishers should be checked regularly to ensure that they are in good working order and the contents are intact. A small stick-on label should show the date of the last inspection.

Accidents at work

Most accidents at work can be avoided. Many are the result of carelessness and include

- trapping and cutting fingers
- walking into doors
- falling down steps
- lifting heavy objects
- insect stings or bites
- minor electric shocks.

Larger companies may employ nurses but most organisations have a list of qualified **first aiders** who can give first aid assistance.

Although many organisations do not have sick rooms, every workplace and office should have a **first aid box**. Drugs are *never* kept in first aid boxes and should not be offered to people who are feeling unwell.

Check the contents of the first aid box in your organisation. Make a list of the items and discuss the contents with your tutor.

Details of all accidents should be recorded in an **accident book**.

Typical entries would look like this.

Date	Time	Name of injured person	How did accident happen?	Details of injury and treatment given	Name of witness	Was accident report form completed? Yes/No
6 May	9.30	Clare Taylor	Trapped hand in door	Hand swollen – taken to hosp.	Ken Page	Yes
9 May	2.00	Jason Kent	Cut finger opening package	Small cut – plaster applied	Sue Lund	No

Depending on the policy of the organisation, often an **accident report form** is also completed. This form is filed away and may need to be referred to if the injured person makes a claim against the company in respect of the injuries sustained.

Your tutor will give you a blank accident report form (page 189). Read through all the questions on this form before looking at the details of an accident given below. When you have familiarised yourself with these details, complete the accident report form, paying particular attention to accuracy and neatness.

Accident details

Matthew Kingston, aged 28, from the Accounts Department, slipped down the stairs whilst leaving the canteen. He grazed his back quite badly and injured his thumb whilst trying to save himself. He was taken to the first aid room by Simon Walker, who was with him at the time of the accident, but it was decided to take him to hospital for an X-ray on his thumb. His arm was put in a sling to ease the pain.

The accident happened today at 1.15 pm. Matthew's home address is 15 Tenby Close, Bridgtown.

After completing the form, you should sign it as the person reporting the accident and date with today's date.

Fill in the missing letters and then write the completed words in your folder to help you remember what they mean.

1 _x__ngui_h__s are supplied in different sizes and colours and contain special liquids for fighting fires.

2 Employees should go through a period of in__ct___ when beginning a new job.

3 Drugs should never be kept in the __rs_ a__ b_x.

4 When a person is injured at work, a record should be made in the _ccid__t _oo_.

5 Buckets of sand, fire b___k_t_ and extinguishers are types of fire fighting equipment.

6 When the fire alarm is sounded, everyone should _v_c__te the building.

7 Plasters, b_nd_g_s and scissors are some of the items which are kept in the first aid box.

8 Buildings are evacuated in the event of fires or b_m_ th____s.

9 The contents of fire extinguishers can be identified by their c_l_u_.

10 The person appointed to look after the safety in your building is called the s_f_t_ _e_r_s_nta_ive.

Wordsearch

Look at the grid shown below and find the following words.

EVACUATION

BLANKET

EXTINGUISHER

SAND

PROCEDURE

BANDAGES

ALARM

CHEMICAL

INJURY

INDUCTION

E	E	C	H	E	M	I	C	A	L	R	R
P	P	R	O	C	E	D	U	R	E	N	E
T	E	G	H	F	F	B	I	U	O	B	H
Y	O	V	W	X	G	H	W	I	V	L	S
Q	A	L	A	R	M	F	T	B	S	A	I
Y	F	P	R	C	S	C	H	E	C	N	U
R	T	Y	Y	U	U	C	G	L	P	K	G
U	S	A	N	D	W	A	L	P	T	E	N
J	W	Q	N	L	D	T	T	I	Y	T	I
N	X	I	Q	N	I	P	L	I	W	Q	T
I	S	W	A	B	R	T	M	F	O	S	X
Q	W	B	F	W	A	M	Y	O	R	N	E

2.3 Contribute to maintaining the security of the workplace and its contents

This section covers

▶ security procedures
  – premises
  – equipment
  – information
▶ unauthorised persons.

Security procedures

Premises

Many organisations are becoming increasingly security conscious. They either employ their own security staff or contract an outside firm to provide security guards. Their duties can include

● checking all visitors arriving at the entrance and issuing security badges
● keeping the car park under surveillance for vandalism and unauthorised parking (Sometimes all registration numbers of delivery vehicles are noted to establish proof of transit of goods in and out of the company.)
● providing a safe escort for staff who deal with or collect cash
● checking that all exits and windows are secured.

Can you list at least *ten* shops or organisations which now employ their own security personnel?

More and more companies now have security VDU screens positioned in various parts of the building which enable reception staff or security guards to monitor the building but yet remain unobtrusive.

Video cameras can be positioned to cover a wide area of the car park and outside areas.

Colleges, town halls, libraries and other public organisations employ security staff to protect their employees against violent incidents which, unfortunately, have increased in recent years.

Specially toughened glass screens (sometimes bullet-proof) are installed to protect staff from aggressive callers (e.g. banks, DSS offices). Employers can install panic buttons which staff can press to summon help in an emergency. The majority of businesses now have burglar alarms to deter intruders and vandals. These alarms can be directly linked to the Police Station. Occasionally, guard dogs are left inside the business compound to deter intruders.

For bomb threats by telephone – see page 68.

Equipment

It is important that staff follow basic security procedures to prevent valuable equipment from being mislaid or stolen. Precautions could include

- typewriters, TVs, video recorders, computers, fax machines etc. all marked invisibly with a special marker pen to help identification if stolen
- mobile telephones, lap top computers, audio tape recorders and other small items locked away securely when not being used
- cupboards, filing cabinets and desk drawers locked at the end of each day
- petty cash box not left lying around unlocked, and only certain people having access to the petty cash
- the main office safe kept locked at all times.

Remember: It is no good locking cupboards, then leaving the keys lying around!

Deterrents to would-be intruders could be

- cash till drawers left wide open overnight to show there is no cash inside (Sometimes more damage is caused by breaking into the till.)
- notices stating that there is no cash left on the premises overnight.

Unfortunately, businesses lose many small items and consumables because *employees* help themselves.

The stationery cupboard or stock room should be kept locked and items of stationery should only be issued to staff against an authorised requisition.

Employees should not take small amounts of paper, envelopes, pens, pencils, correcting liquid etc. for their personal use. This is **pilfering** and can lead to disciplinary action being taken!

Information

Much of the information which businesses deal with is confidential and steps should be taken to prevent unauthorised people having access to it.

Keep confidential files in lockable filing cabinets, with keys issued only to those persons who should have access to them.

Data on people which is kept on computer is covered by the Data Protection Act (see page 95).

Other types of computer data, such as financial information and wages or salaries can be kept secure by

- denying access to people without a password†
- computer users changing passwords frequently
- creating various levels of access to data by only giving certain employees the relevant password (e.g. directors' salaries can only be accessed by one senior wages clerk)
- some computer programs can be set up so that it is possible to check which persons have had access to them during the previous 24 hours.

†When passwords are keyed in, nothing actually appears on screen. This prevents anyone discovering your password.

Remember: Do not throw confidential computer print-outs into the waste bin where they may be read by other people.

Computer files can also be protected by taking back-up copies of files at the end of each day (sometimes more frequently) in case of computer breakdown. Back-up copies are invaluable if the original disks are damaged, stolen or misplaced. Because of the risk of fire, back-up copies should be stored in a fire proof cabinet or, ideally, in a separate building.

Viruses can be introduced to computer programs either intentionally or by accident. If your computer is displaying a virus notice, the computer and all disks which have been used in the machine should be 'swept'.

Unauthorised persons

In many companies now, each employee is issued with an identity card incorporating their name and photograph which must be worn at all times. The card could incorporate a bar code which enables the holder to gain access to designated areas.

Details of all visitors should be recorded by reception and, if applicable, the visitor may be given a badge to wear. They should be escorted to the person they have called to see unless they are regular callers.

Alternatively, visitors can be collected by secretaries coming down to reception.

Workmen should be asked for proof of identity and, if this is not forthcoming, a telephone check can be made to their employer.

You should be vigilant in the following ways.

- Challenge all strangers. Ask, 'Can I help you?'
- Ask to see proof of identity of any stranger or workman you feel uneasy about.
- Never leave visitors alone in your office where they could read confidential information.
- Do not leave money, handbags or jackets lying around.
- Do not disclose confidential information to strangers.

SECTION REVIEW

Fill in the gaps in the following sentences. Choose only one of the two words shown at the end of each sentence.

1 When keying in a _____, nothing appears on screen. (**password**, **program**)

2 Disks will need to be swept if a computer _____ is discovered. (**germ**, **virus**)

3 Some businesses try to deter intruders by leaving the cash till drawer _____ overnight. (**closed**, **open**)

4 Marking equipment with an invisible ink _____ can help identification when the article is found. (**pen**, **pencil**)

5 Identity badges incorporating _____ are now becoming increasingly popular with companies. (**photographs**, **fingerprints**)

6 Computer users should change passwords _____ . (**annually**, **frequently**)

7 Workmen, without proof of their _____ should not be admitted. (**qualifications**, **identity**)

8 _____ buttons enable staff to summon help in an emergency. (**information**, **panic**)

9 Computer data on personnel is covered by the _____ _____ Act. (**Data Protection**, **Computer Data**)

10 _____ files should be kept in a locked filing cabinet. (**confidential**, **overdue**)

Crossword

Across

1 Abbreviation for computer screen (3)
6 Equipment installed to deter intruders (5)
7 Visitors could be asked to wear one (5)
9 Must not be left lying around (4)
10 This type of person should be challenged (12)
11 All visitors should report here first (9)

Down

2 Type of animal used for security patrol (3)
3 Must be changed frequently (8)
4 Another word for information (4)
5 Equipment used to monitor car parks (6)
8 They should be closed every night (7)
10 Computer _____ could be denied access (4)

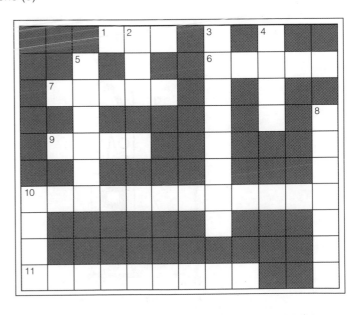

3.1 Follow instructions and operate equipment

This section covers

▶ understanding instructions
▶ operating procedures
  – reprographic equipment
  – computers, printers and typewriters
  – communicating equipment.

Understanding instructions

> 'Owing to the sophisticated nature of the circuitry and mechanisms utilised in the printer, operator's troubleshooting is logically obliged to be limited to certain easily recognisable symptoms and cures.'

What does this gobbledegook mean?

Well, believe it or not, this is an extract from a manual about printers!

Wouldn't it have been clearer to say:

> 'Because of the complicated workings of the printer, operators will only be able to deal with easily recognisable faults.'

Fortunately, most instructions manuals which are supplied with office equipment these days are written in clear, easy to understand language.

Many of the instructions are explained in graphic form, enabling the operator to understand instructions quickly without having to read lengthy paragraphs.

What messages are the following illustrations giving you?

1   2

3   4

5   6

7 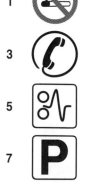   8

9   10

An instruction booklet is always supplied with any type of office equipment. this booklet usually gives detailed instructions about some or all of the following

- setting up or assembling the equipment
- safety procedures
- a diagram identifying various parts of the equipment
- how to carry out the various functions
- replacing consumables and other parts
- what to do when things go wrong (usually called **troubleshooting**)
- suggestions for cleaning and maintenance of the equipment
- an index for easy reference.

Graphic illustrations are often used to simplify written instructions. e.g.

Avoid placing your photocopier

in direct sunlight   on an uneven surface

in a dusty area   noar strong vibrations.

Keep the instruction booklet supplied with the equipment in a safe place. You should take a photocopy of the booklet in case of loss.

An initial demonstration of the equipment by the supplying company is usually given free of charge when it is delivered and installed. You should not hesitate to clarify any part of the operating procedure with the demonstrator.

It is important that operators follow instructions when using the equipment, as failure to do so can result in the manufacturer's warranty becoming invalid.

Remember: Learn to follow instructions, particularly those laid down by your organisation. This will ensure good working practices and will help to prevent accidents in the workplace.

For safety legislation in the workplace, see page 19.

If you lost your direction whilst travelling along the motorway, wouldn't you check the route on a map rather than guess which direction to take?

'Mrs Pearson said, "Turn left after the 149th traffic cone".'

It **makes sense** to check with your supervisor or refer to the manufacturer's manual if you are experiencing problems with any type of office equipment.

Operating procedures

Because instructions for using different types of equipment vary from machine to machine, you must check the operating procedure for the machine you are using either from the operator's manual or with your supervisor.

Reprographic equipment

Find out how to carry out the following functions using the reprographic equipment in your office or college.

- Take an A4 copy.
- Reduce an A4 copy to A5 size.
- Enlarge an A4 copy on to A3 size paper.
- Take a back-to-back copy (double-sided).
- Collate multi-pages.
- Copy two opposite pages from an open book (using book mode facility).
- Copy on to an OHP transparency.
- Refill the paper tray.
- Replace the toner (powder or cartridge).
- Empty used toner.

What other functions can be carried out on your equipment? Make a note of how to do them.

Computers, printers and typewriters

Find out how to carry out the following functions on your working equipment.

Computer
- Log on (using a password, if applicable).
- Select a software program from the menu.
- Exit from the program after use.
- Log off correctly.

Printer
- Reload with paper, aligned correctly for printing.
- Take a print out.
- Change the printer ribbon.

Typewriter
- Identify various parts (by referring to illustrations in the operator's booklet).
- Load paper, set margins and tabs.
- Operate basic functions (deletion, centring, indent etc.).
- Check for additional functions.

Communicating equipment

Telephones, answering machines, fax machines

Find out how to carry out the following functions on the equipment in your office or college.

Telephone
- Answer an incoming call.
- Put the caller on hold.
- Transfer the caller to another extension.
- Contact your switchboard operator.
- Make an outgoing call.

Answering machine
- Set up the tape to take incoming calls.
- Rewind tape to listen to recorded messages.

Fax machine
- Send a single page or multi-page message by fax.
- Use the telephone handset during transmission.
- Make a photocopy on the machine.
- Insert a new fax paper roll or reload with paper.

General do's and don'ts

Do

- ✔ Switch off electricity before opening machinery.
- ✔ Use only recommended replacement parts.
- ✔ Switch off the machine if it becomes overheated.
- ✔ Check with the instruction manual if unsure of any of the functions.

Don't

✘ Put drinks on or near equipment.
✘ Balance equipment on the edge of desks.
✘ Rest heavy objects on top of equipment.
✘ Allow sharp objects to scratch the exposure glass of a photocopier.
✘ Carry heavy equipment – use a trolley if it has to be moved.
✘ Keep equipment in direct sunlight.
✘ Allow anything to rest on the power cable.
✘ Leave wires trailing.
✘ Allow small objects such as paper clips to fall into the equipment.

How good are you at giving clear instructions?

Select *one* of either the **do's** or **don'ts** from above and design an **illustration** which would explain your chosen instruction clearly.

Your design could be in cartoon form if you prefer.

You may add a caption underneath but do not use more than *six* words.

Ask your tutor to judge whose illustration is best!

Look at the diagrams below which all relate to the care of floppy disks.
Write down what you think each illustration is telling you.

Care of floppy disks
Never

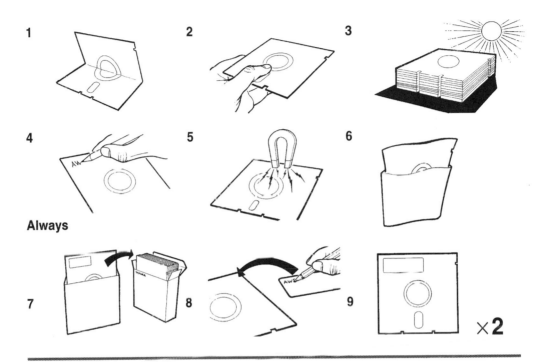

Always

×**2**

Wordsearch

Look at the grid below and find the missing words.

ILLUSTRATE

DIAGRAM

GOBBLEDEGOOK

MAINTENANCE

INSTRUCTION

FAULT

OPERATE

ELECTRICITY

OVERHEAT

FLOPPY

Y	P	P	O	L	F	G	R	W	O	B	K
T	I	N	S	T	R	U	C	T	I	O	N
I	Z	X	W	Q	H	K	M	D	O	T	O
C	G	G	H	U	F	A	N	G	O	F	V
I	V	N	V	S	R	X	E	V	P	A	E
R	E	Q	P	G	M	D	O	P	E	U	R
T	C	X	A	B	E	M	T	Y	R	L	H
C	W	I	L	L	U	S	T	R	A	T	E
E	D	C	B	W	I	P	W	B	T	Q	A
L	G	B	V	C	F	Q	L	P	E	C	T
E	O	S	V	B	R	E	Y	U	E	W	J
G	M	A	I	N	T	E	N	A	N	C	E

3.2 Keep equipment in a clean and working condition

This section covers

▶ maintenance procedures
  - reprographic equipment
  - computers, printers and typewriters
  - communicating equipment

▶ replacing consumables
▶ disposal of waste items

Maintenance procedures

When reprographic equipment is covered by a maintenance agreement, many problems can be solved simply by sending for the engineer. However, the machine operator must take some responsibility for keeping equipment in good working order.

Reprographic equipment

Regular maintenance should include

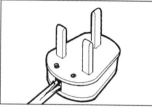

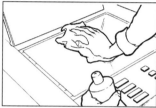

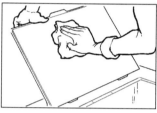

- inspecting electric plugs and wiring for wear and tear

- cleaning the exposure glass with a soft cloth and glass cleaner to remove dirty marks

- cleaning the platen cover with a damp cloth

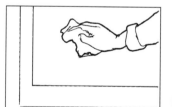

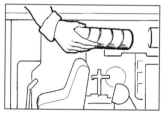

- cleaning the exterior of the equipment with a damp cloth and weak cleaning solution to remove stubborn marks

- refilling paper trays – fan paper first to separate sheets

- replacing toner if copies are becoming faint.

Computers, printers and typewriters

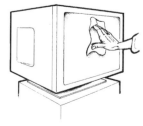

Regular maintenance should include

- checking electric plugs and cables for wear
- dusting the outer parts with a soft cloth
- cleaning the keyboard using a soft brush to dislodge particles between the keys
- wiping the platen roller with a weak solution of spirit to prevent shine
- replacing ribbon cassettes and correcting tapes when required
- cleaning VDU screens with anti-static spray or wipes.

Communicating equipment

Telephones, answering machines, fax machines

Because telephone equipment is usually used by more than one person, it is important that the handset, **particularly the mouthpiece**, is kept clean. Sterilised wipes are available with which the handset can be cleaned regularly.

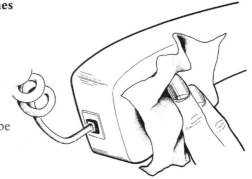

Other types of communicating equipment should be kept dust free by wiping them with a dry cloth. Stubborn marks can be removed by using a damp cloth and a weak cleaning solution.

Again, a regular check must be made to electric cabling and plugs.

Replacing consumables

Looking after equipment must include replacing consumable items when necessary. Always keep a small supply nearby, for immediate replacement

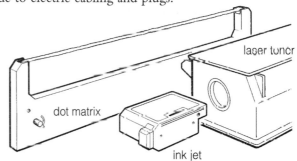

laser toner

dot matrix

ink jet

The equipment in your office consists of the following.

| Photocopier | Electronic typewriter | Fax machine | Microcomputer | Dot matrix printer |

Your supervisor has asked you to tidy the consumables cupboard and label each item with the type of equipment for which it is intended.

Can you complete the list below?

You may decide that the same consumable item can be used for more than one machine. The first one is completed for you.

Listing paper	_Dot matrix printer_	**A4 bond paper**	_____
Glass cleaner	_____	**Paper rolls**	_____
Batteries	_____	**Photocopy paper**	_____
Letter head paper	_____	**Ribbon cassettes**	_____
Toner	_____	**Correction tapes**	_____
Daisy wheel	_____		
Carbon paper	_____	**OHP transparencies**	_____
Disk box	_____	**Floppy disks**	_____

It is important that each consumable item is clearly marked with the type of equipment for which it is intended, e.g. ribbon cassettes would be stocked for typewriters *and* printers.

Did you realise this, when completing the list in the last task?

Disposal of waste items

Rubbish

Fires love rubbish. Get rubbish out of your premises as quickly and as often as possible.

Many businesses now separate clean, waste paper, which is sent for recycling, but care must be exercised when storing this type of paper.

If rubbish must be burned, keep it well away from buildings in case flying sparks cause a real fire. Use a proper incinerator, site it well way from buildings and stand guard over it.

Smoking

Smoking is still one of the most frequent causes of fires starting.

Designate an area where staff may smoke.

Last thing in the evening, check that no cigarette ends have been left burning. Empty all ashtrays regularly.

Dangerous goods

Some waste items, particularly those of an explosive or flammable nature, must be disposed of with special care.

Aerosols, gas cartridges and cylinders can explode and start fires if exposed to heat.

Toner powder from photocopiers can cause flashback when exposed to an open flame.

Corrosive liquids, such as acid and thinners, can damage surfaces of furniture and machinery.

All flammable chemicals should be labelled clearly and stored in a well-ventilated room, well away from any source of heat.

Clear instructions should be displayed in case of spillage.

For COSHH regulations, see page 19.
For PPE regulations, see page 21.

Fill in the gaps in the following sentences. Choose only *one* of the two words shown at the end of each sentence.

1 Telephone handsets should be cleaned regularly to prevent _____. (**faults, germs**)

2 Clean all keyboards with a _____ brush. (**soft, stiff**)

3 The _____ glass on a photocopier should be cleaned daily. (**exposure, exterior**)

4 Use a _____ cleaning solution to remove stubborn marks from the exterior of office equipment. (**weak, strong**)

5 All consumable items should be _____ clearly. (**labelled, listed**)

6 Paper for fax machines is supplied in _____. (**bales, rolls**)

7 A _____ wheel can be found on an electronic typewriter. (**petal, daisy**)

8 Telephones, fax and answering machines are types of _____ equipment. (**copying, communicating**)

9 Used _____ should be disposed of safely. (**toner, powder**)

10 The safety legislation governing the control of hazardous substances is known as _____. (**HASAWA, COSHH**)

Crossword

Across

2 A consumable item (6)
4 Electricity fault – check _____ (4)
7 Safety regulations covering hazardous substances (5)
9 Regular maintenance _____ should be made to wiring (6)
10 Daisy _____ (5)

Down

1 Call him to remedy machine breakdown (8)
3 Used for cleaning keyboards (5)
5 Consumables for micros (5)
6 Replace if copies become faint (5)
8 Type of transparency (3)

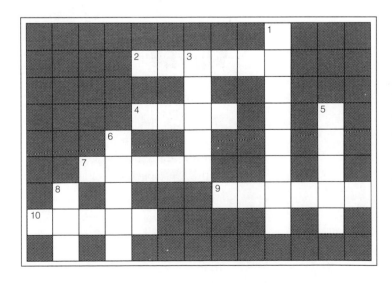

4 Develop effective working relationships

4.1 Create and maintain effective working relationships with other members of staff

This section covers

▶ working with and assisting business colleagues
▶ difficulties in working relationships
▶ communicating with senior staff
▶ colleagues with special needs
▶ grievance and disciplinary procedures
▶ Equal Opportunities legislation.

Working with and assisting business colleagues

> **Be honest!**
>
> Do you get on with every person you work with or everybody in your class?

Probably very few people can answer 'yes'.

'I can't help Joanna check these figures, Mrs Pearson, 'cos I'm not speaking to her this week!'

There are two reasons why it is important for employees to get on with each other.

● At least 36 hours a week are spent at work and this can seem a very long time if relationships with other people are strained.
● Your employer is not going to get 100 per cent effort from people who cannot work well together.

Employees who have a good working relationship and enjoy each other's company will generally like going to work. When relations are strained, this can lead to people staying off sick or even looking for alternative employment.

There are several ways in which you can assist the work flow in your office, particularly when deadlines have to be met.

- Ask colleagues who are *obviously* under pressure if you can help them.
- Offer to do the more routine tasks for your senior colleagues.
- Answer the telephone and deal with callers, to avoid busy colleagues being disturbed.
- Be prepared to work on for those few extra minutes into your lunch break, or at the end of the day, if this will enable a job to be completed.
- Do not show resentment when colleagues ask for your assistance. (Your annoyance can be easily identified by your body language.)
- Make the tea or coffee when colleagues are too busy – even though it is not your turn!

Remember: Your willingness to help and assist others will not go unnoticed by senior colleagues.

Difficulties in working relationships

Difficulties can arise in many ways and it is important to recognise how these can occur. Reasons could include:

- one person not pulling their weight – continually trying to avoid jobs
- not being willing to work as part of a team
- continually producing inaccurate, sloppy work
- unnecessarily trying to gain favour with senior staff
- not bothering to take or pass on messages to colleagues
- continually arriving late and wanting to leave early
- taking excessive sick leave
- discussing one colleague with another
- staff competing with one another for promotion
- not sharing *all* jobs e.g. tea-making, washing cups, errands
- starting, and passing on, malicious gossip.

Can you honestly say that none of the above reasons applies to you?

Remember: You don't necessarily have to like colleagues – just get on with them!

If you are ever in the wrong, have the courage to admit and apologise. It will prevent a lot of unpleasantness.

Communicating with senior staff

There is nothing more embarrassing for an employer or supervisor than an employee being over-familiar.

When starting a new job, you should try to assess how senior staff will expect you to behave towards them.

Tips to follow

- Watch how other staff on your level relate to people in authority.
- Address seniors with a title e.g. 'Mr Parkinson', 'Mrs Bennett' until you are invited to use their first name.
- Politely respond to general conversation without becoming too chatty.
- *Never* ask personal questions, 'What does your wife think about this?', 'How much did that cost you?'
- Be discreet. Never gossip about anything which is said to you in confidence.
- Avoid running down colleagues and tale-telling to senior staff. The consequences of this could be quite serious – for you!

Colleagues with special needs

Consideration should be shown to colleagues with special needs by

- speaking to deaf people face to face, to enable them to lip-read
- reaching articles for physically handicapped colleagues who would find them difficult to reach otherwise
- keeping pathways and corridors clear for blind people and moving obstacles which they may be unaware of
- explaining instructions slowly to people with limited ability (Do not attempt to show them too much at once. Wait until they have mastered the basics before proceeding to give further instruction.)
- temporarily giving extra help to colleagues with broken limbs – but *only* until they are fully mobile again!

Grievance and disciplinary procedures

When beginning employment with a company, all employees should be given (within thirteen weeks of starting work) a **contract of employment** which sets out clearly the terms and conditions of employment.

The contract will outline the procedure to follow in the event of the employee having a grievance at work, or if the company feels the employee should be disciplined for breaking one of the rules of the organisation.

If an employee feels they have been unfairly treated, they should first talk to their immediate supervisor to see if the problem can be resolved. If this fails, the employee can take the dispute to a higher level, who will obtain more evidence to check the facts of the grievance. The **Union** could become involved at this stage to give support to the employee.

The outcome of the grievance procedure should be notified in writing to the employee.

If an employer feels that an employee should be disciplined (e.g. for arriving late for work regularly, unsatisfactory work, sexual harassment) they can be warned verbally by their supervisor.

If the problem persists, the employee can be given a written warning which sets out details of the offence and states what their future conduct is expected to be.

A further final written warning could result in dismissal.

Equal Opportunities legislation

Many companies now are describing themselves as **Equal Opportunities Employers**. What does this mean?

- The company will have an **equal opportunity policy**. This is a document setting out the company's plans for hiring and promoting staff fairly and not discriminating against anyone on the grounds of gender (male or female), ethnic background or disability.
- The **Equal Opportunities Commission**, a public body set up in 1975, has stated that it is unlawful to discriminate on the grounds of gender and that men and women should be given equal opportunities at work.
- The **Race Relations Act 1976** forbids discrimination against any person on the grounds of colour, race, nationality or ethnic or racial origin.
- The **Sex Discrimination Act 1975** makes unlawful any job advertisement which shows preference for either a man or a woman.
- Promotion opportunities should be available equally to both men and women.

Bias against women

❝Women can't work under the pressure which this job demands.❞

❝How would you feel about having to walk through the factory, where all the employees are men?❞

❝When do you intend to start a family?❞

Bias against men

❝We need someone with a sympathetic and caring approach, and that means a woman.❞

❝Do you think you could cope with working in a mainly female environment?❞

Discuss with your tutor any examples of unlawful bias which have been previously experienced by yourself or any members of your group.

Fill in the missing letters and then write the completed words in your folder to help you remember them.

1 Requests from colleagues should be responded to w_ll__g_y.

2 Offer assistance to colleagues so that d__dl_n_s can be kept to.

3 Men and women should be given e___l opportunities for promotion.

4 It is important to be able to c___un_c_te with senior staff.

5 Speaking face to face with a d__f person will enable them to lip-read.

6 It is important for co__eag__s to work well together.

7 To maintain good working relationships, staff should not pass on malicious __ss_p.

8 Staff who are in the wrong should have the courage to ap___gis_.

9 When addressing senior staff for the first time, you should use a courtesy t___e.

10 It is unlawful to d_sc___in_te on the grounds of sex.

Wordsearch

Look at the grid shown below and find the following words.

CLEAN

CALLERS

WORKLOAD

DRESS

COLLEAGUE

IMAGE

DISCREET

POLITE

STANDARDS

BEHAVIOUR

H	C	O	L	L	E	A	G	U	E	Y
S	F	G	U	G	K	P	A	D	T	N
G	C	E	A	T	P	O	U	R	T	R
C	X	M	P	U	O	T	U	E	E	C
G	I	B	F	D	L	O	R	S	E	A
G	U	O	G	H	I	K	O	S	R	L
F	S	H	T	V	T	U	R	F	C	L
C	L	E	A	N	E	B	V	H	S	E
F	E	H	T	G	H	R	E	W	I	R
K	E	S	T	A	N	D	A	R	D	S
B	K	U	W	O	R	K	L	O	A	D

4.2 Greet and assist visitors

This section covers

- location and responsibilities of colleagues
- types of caller
- greeting callers
- non-verbal communications
- difficult callers
- callers with special needs
- dealing with delays/non-availability
- escorting callers to destinations
- confidentiality
- security.

The receptionist is usually the first point of contact which most visitors have with an organisation. The way in which visitors are dealt with by the receptionist creates an image of the company which is very important if it is to attract new customers and keep existing customers satisfied.

Location and responsibilities of colleagues

It is important that the receptionist is fully aware of the work and responsibilities of each department and, more especially, where colleagues can be found. There is nothing more annoying for visitors than to be kept waiting because the receptionist is unsure about which person can best deal with the matter. This situation can be avoided if

- a list of expected callers, with appointments, is given to the receptionist each morning
- the internal telephone list is kept up to date (particularly if colleagues have moved into different offices)
- staff who leave the building make sure that the receptionist is kept informed of their absence and their expected time of return
- the receptionist is kept informed of any newspaper advertisements, or promotions, which may produce enquiries from the public
- the receptionist is informed on a daily basis of any colleagues who are away, either on business or through sickness.

Types of caller

Throughout each day, many callers may visit your office. They could include

- visitors with appointments
- people without appointments
- customers paying bills
- sales representatives
- new customers making enquiries about products
- people making enquiries about job vacancies
- postmen/women
- delivery persons
- people performing a service e.g. milkman, repairmen
- friends and relations of colleagues.

All these people will form an instant opinion of your company by the way and manner in which you deal with them.

Greeting callers

Look at how the receptionist dealt with the *seven* callers below, then write down how you would have responded to each caller.

- **Person enquiring about a job vacancy**
  'We have some application forms somewhere but I just can't find them. Can you call back tomorrow?'

- **New customers**
  'Yes, what do you want?'

- **Photocopier engineer**
  'I hope your van isn't blocking anybody in on the car park. You won't be too popular!'

- **Customer paying a bill of £20.10 with three £10 notes**
  'You're going to take all our small change!'

- **Visitor with appointment**
  'You'll have to wait. Mr Fairhurst is still dictating some letters to his secretary.'

- **Sales representative**
  'We have a very strict rule which I am not allowed to break. Sales reps are only seen on Wednesdays and Fridays by appointment.'

- **Customer enquiring about a product**
  'I don't really know much about this item. I haven't a clue how it works.'

Discuss with your tutor and the other members of your group how you would have responded.

Non-verbal communications

Remember, callers do not necessarily have to communicate verbally with you in order to transmit information. The way they look at you, move, and the expression on their faces can let you know what they are thinking or feeling.

The actions of *four* different callers are described below. Match each one against the descriptions shown in the end column.

1	Reluctant to approach the desk, looks round continually.	**A** *angry*
2	Taps on the desk for your attention whilst you are dealing with another caller.	**B** *pleasant*
3	Glares at you whilst waiting for attention.	**C** *nervous*
4	Smiles warmly at you whilst approaching the desk.	**D** *impatient*

Have you decided which description matches the actions of each of the four callers?

These signals are called **non-verbal communications**. They tell you a lot about callers before you actually speak to them. You must learn how to interpret these signals.

Remember: The signals you give out will tell callers a lot about you!

Difficult callers

Angry, aggressive caller

- Be polite and patient.
- Listen without interrupting.
- Get help if you cannot deal with the situation yourself.

Shy, nervous caller

- Try to put them at ease with a friendly smile.
- Listen carefully to what they have to say.
- Give any information slowly and quietly – repeating it for them if necessary.

Callers without appointments

- Use your common sense here. If you think there is a possibility of the caller being seen, discreetly make enquiries.
- Otherwise, offer to make an appointment.
- For persistent reps, ask them to make an appointment, or accept their business card to pass on.

Callers making collections

- Check what the policy of your company is about making donations. They can become a nuisance.

People who want to stay and chat

- Often they are friends or relatives waiting for one of your colleagues.
- Try to discourage them from taking up too much of your time.
- Offer them a seat away from your desk, direct them to the washroom, give them a magazine.
- If all this fails – politely say how you would love to chat but you have too much work to do!

Callers with special needs

Some callers may be physically handicapped, others may need extra consideration.

Older, less mobile callers

Avoid asking them to climb stairs if possible. Find out if the person who they have called to see can come down to reception.

Disabled callers

Again, it may be possible for them to be seen in a downstairs room, near reception. Otherwise, escort them by opening doors and allowing extra time to take them to their appointment room.

Deaf or partially deaf callers

Speak face to face with them, more slowly than usual, so they can lip-read. There is no need to shout – this can be very embarrassing for them.

Blind callers

Speak directly to them, so they can locate you. Gently take their arm when escorting them to their appointment, pointing out steps and other obstacles.

Callers with special mobility needs

Many companies now have special facilities for those people with special mobility needs. These can include

- automatic doors
- ramps for wheelchair access
- toilet facilities for the disabled
- lifts with easily-reached controls
- extra-wide doorways in corridors.

The receptionist should be alert to the requirements of the less mobile and offer assistance where necessary.

Callers with limited mental ability

Be patient whilst they explain their reason for calling. Give any instructions clearly, without complication. Be prepared to explain more than once if necessary. Give directions very clearly or escort them personally to the person they have come to see. Do not be patronising.

Foreign visitors

Much will depend upon their command of the English language. It may be necessary to explain things several times.

Dealing with delays/non-availability

If there is a delay in callers being attended to

- If possible, explain the reason for the delay.
- Ask them to sit down – do not leave them standing.
- Offer tea/coffee or a magazine.
- Direct them to the washroom, if required.
- Reassure them regularly that they have not been forgotten.
- After ten minutes, remind the member of staff that the caller is still waiting.
- Try to make occasional conversation with them, without interrupting your work routine – 'Have you travelled far?'
- When they can eventually be seen, be sure to apologise for the delay.

If it is not possible for the caller to be dealt with

- Explain the reason fully e.g., 'Mr Watts is away in London until tomorrow.'
- See if anyone else could deal with the matter.

- Offer to pass on a message, provide a notepad and pen, if required.
- Make an appointment for a later date.
- Pass a message to the member of staff concerned informing them of the caller's visit.

Escorting callers to destinations

Moving visitors from reception to another part of the building will depend upon the procedure operated by the company.

Callers may

- be given directions to the place of their appointment
- be collected by the person they have come to see or by a secretary
- be escorted by a member of the office or security staff.

Whilst escorting visitors, make polite conversation with them, open doors for them and point out any hazards to be avoided. Introduce visitors to the person they have called to see, if they are not already known.

General rules for introductions are

- Introduce a man to a woman.
  'Miss Armstrong, this is Mr Parker, our Sales Manager.'
- Introduce a younger woman to an older one.
- Introduce a younger man to an older one.
- When introducing a husband and wife, mention them both.
  'Mr Blake, this is Mr and Mrs Wilton, Mr and Mrs Wilton, this is Mr Blake, our Accountant.'
- When introducing a visitor to a group of people, introduce the individual first.
  'Mrs Clarkson, this is Mr Baker, Mr Kent and Mr Slater. Gentlemen, meet Mrs Clarkson.'

Confidentiality

If one of your duties is to attend to callers, follow these guidelines.

- *Never* disclose any confidential information about the company or the staff who work there. If you are unsure about what you may disclose, *ask* someone more senior!
- *Do not* discuss personal or financial matters with callers when other visitors can listen. Offer some degree of privacy.
- Take care when speaking on the telephone in a reception area. *Make sure* visitors do not overhear private information.

Finally, do not gossip!

Security

For larger companies, security begins in the car park. Security guards will record car registration numbers and issue badges to visitors. Different coloured badges may indicate access only to specified areas.

Further checks should be made on casual callers.

Callers may be asked to leave baggage with the guards to be collected on departure.

Visitors are often asked to complete and sign a **Visitors' register** or **Callers' log** giving their name, company and details of their visit.

VISITORS' REGISTER						
					Date ..*12 May 199–*............	
Time	Caller's name	Company	Car Reg No	Called to see	Business	Time of departure
0900	John Dean	Brightwell Industries	L413TKY	Peter Kay	Advertising contact	1015
0915	Susan Kent	–	–	Jean Bond	Job interview	1000
1020	L Seymour	Seymour Commercials	M318LBX	G Pointer	Transport	1115

The visitor's badge will be handed back when departing.

Because of recent incidents of explosives being found in public places, many companies do not allow callers to move out of the reception area. Members of staff will come down to reception to conduct any business there.

Generally, several interview rooms are available. This eliminates the need for callers to wander around the building unescorted.

All staff should

- close and lock all windows after use
- keep offices locked when not occupied
- never leave handbags or jackets on desks and chairs unattended – lock them away out of sight
- never leave cash on desks unattended
- lock office doors when counting money e.g. wages, banking
- keep a look-out for unattended bags or parcels left on the premises
- challenge any unauthorised person seen on the premises (particularly if acting suspiciously).

SECTION REVIEW

Use the following words, *once* only, to complete the sentences below.

confidential   register
delay   introducing
security   greeting
difficult   image
appointments   escort

1 A suitable_____ to visitors would be 'Good morning, can I help you?'

2 If there is a _____ in a member of staff keeping an appointment, the visitor could be offered refreshments.

3 An efficient receptionist should give a good _____ of the company.

4 Certain courtesy rules should be followed when _____ visitors to the person they have come to see.

5 As a _____ measure, a note is often made of visitors' car registration numbers.

6 It is advisable to _____ callers from reception to the person they have called to see.

7 Tact should be used when dealing with _____ callers.

8 Sales representatives should be encouraged to make _____ rather then just call hoping to see the Sales Manager.

9 When speaking on the telephone, in the presence of visitors, you must take care not to disclose _____ matters.

10 In many companies, visitors are asked to sign a _____.

Crossword

Across

1 The receptionist should create a good _____ of the company (5)
2 Be on the lookout for these left unattended (4)
4 Rooms not occupied should be kept _____ (6)
6 Callers should be greeted in a _____ manner (6)
7 A caller (7)
8 Sales reps should be encouraged to make one of these (11)

Down

2 An item which visitors may be requested to wear (5)
3 Without speaking, signals given by callers (3) (6)
5 Provided by employing guards (8)
6 The attention all visitors should receive (6)

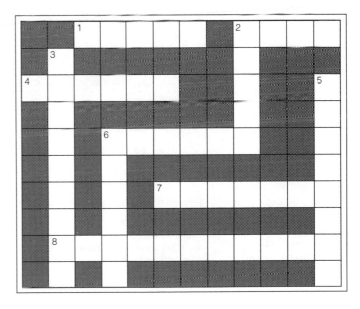

Process information

5.1 Process incoming and outgoing telecommunications

This section covers

- telephone systems
- telephone features
- telephone charge cards
- answering the telephone
- rules for taking messages
- telephone messages
- effective questioning
- passing on information
- making outgoing telephone calls

- confirming telephone arrangements
- answering machines
- telephone reference books
- telephone services
- telephone faults
- telephone charge rates
- emergencies and security procedures
- facsimile transmission
- electronic mail (E-Mail).

A large proportion of business today involves communicating by telephone, fax and E-Mail. Unfortunately, receiving and making telephone calls is probably one of the most dreaded jobs for the inexperienced office worker.

Fears can include

- disconnecting callers by accident
- not being able to transfer a call
- being unable to give the information requested
- having to deal with an angry caller
- getting a message muddled.

It is important therefore that you learn good telephone skills which will enable you to become more confident and efficient.

'I'm really getting the hang of this switchboard, Mrs Pearson. I've only cut seven callers off today.'

Telephone systems

The type of telephone system at your workplace will depend upon the size of your organisation.

Private Automatic Branch Exchange (PABX)

This switchboard will be manned by an operator who answers all incoming calls from a central location.

The operator will transfer calls to other extension users (sometimes well over 100 extensions).

Larger PABXs have **visual display units** (VDUs) enabling the operator to view the whole system on screen at one time.

Multiline or Key Telephone System (KTS)

This system allows all extensions to receive calls, *or* one extension only can act as the switchboard. Although up to 80 extensions can be accommodated, it is usual to have no more than about 25.

Mobile telephones

Mobile telephones are bocoming increasingly popular for use in cars and to carry around. Business people find them invaluable when they are away from the office and women regard them as an additional safety device when travelling alone.

The phones are battery operated and need to be recharged regularly.

Features can include

- LCD screen (liquid crystal display)
- name and number memory
- last number recall
- integral clock, calendar and alarm clock
- low battery warning alarm
- password access to prevent unauthorised use.

Note: Many restaurants and public places discourage the use of mobile telephones because of the disturbance to other clients! They are strictly prohibited on aircraft.

Pagers

Pagers have overtaken bleepers in popularity – in fact, BT have discontinued promoting *Le Bleep*. Modern pagers let your callers send you more than just a bleep.

Depending on the individual model, you can choose from a simple tone alert, a telephone number to ring – displayed on the small screen – or a fully worded message.

Additonal features can include

- 80 character screen display
- illuminated screen
- time and date message stamping
- reminder alert
- clock, calendar and alarm displays
- message file/sort/delete functions.

More sophisticated models can have an answering service linked to a pager which alerts you, by bleeping, that a message has been left for you.

How it works

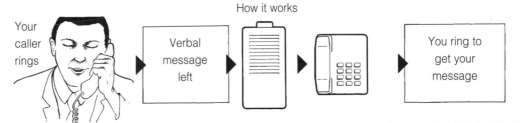

Your caller rings → Verbal message left → You ring to get your message

Telephone features

Many different features are available on modern telephones.

Redial button

Enables you to try the last dialled number again if you could not get through previously,

Liquid crystal display (LCD)

Shows the number you are dialling or recalling from memory on a small screen.

Memories

Frequently called numbers can be put into memory and recalled by pressing a couple of buttons.

Secrecy button

Allows you to speak to someone else in the room without your caller hearing. Just putting your hand over the receiver is not adequate!

Call timer/clock

A display on the phone shows how long each call lasts – useful for keeping costs down! The display acts as a clock when *not* used as a timer.

On-hook dialling

Dial a number – no need to lift the handset until someone answers.

Hands-free operation

A built-in microphone and adjustable loudspeaker allows you to hold a conversation without lifting the handset. Hands are kept free for making notes.

Prompt

If a number is engaged, the phone will store it and three minutes later will bleep to remind you to try it again.

TouchTone phones

If your BT telephone exchange has been modernised, you can have a TouchTone phone. TouchTone phones play notes when you dial and give you faster, clearer connections.

Users have access to the following services for a small rental charge.

Charge advice

After finishing your call, replace the receiver. Your phone will ring and an electronic 'voice' will tell you the cost of the call.

Reminder call

You can book your own alarm call by pressing certain buttons. Calls can also be cancelled.

Call diversion

Your calls can automatically be transferred to another number.

Call waiting

Whilst you are on the phone, a discreet bleep will let you know that another caller is waiting. An option allows you to put your first call on hold whilst you answer the other one.

Three-way calling

Three callers, all on separate telephones, can hold a conversation.

Code calling	Up to 27 frequently called numbers can be stored and redialled by just pressing two buttons.
Repeat last call	Engaged numbers can be redialled automatically by pressing three buttons.
Call barring	Stops people misusing your phone by restricting which numbers can be dialled.

For the disabled or hard of hearing

Additional earpiece	Option of listening to a phone conversation with both ears or allowing someone else to listen in on the additional earpiece, allowing you to lip-read from them.
Call indicator	Light flashes on phone to indicate ringing.
Incoming volume control	The voice of the person calling can be amplified.
Inductive compiler	A device inside the handset assists people who wear hearing aids with a 'T' position to hear more clearly.
Speech amplification	Boosts *your* voice as you speak so the person you are calling can hear you better.

Telephone chargecards

A free plastic card can be obtained, from either British Telecom or Mercury, which can be used when phoning from public pay phones. The charge for the call is simply added to your own home phone bill or business phone bill, for payment later.

This eliminates the need for carrying sufficient coins or having to ask to use someone's private phone.

Chargecards can be used abroad to phone home to the UK, from over 120 countries.

Note: Telephone cards (different from telephone chargecards) can be *bought* in denominations of £2, £4, £10 or £20. Each time the card is used, the number of remaining units decreases, until they are all used up.

Answering the telephone

An incoming call can be

- received direct from an outside line
- transferred to you from your switchboard operator
- transferred to you from another extension.

The tone of the ring will help you to identify whether the call is from an outside line or another extension in your building.

Calls from an outside line should be answered with a greeting and the name of your firm.

'Good morning, Sutcliffe & Jones Solicitors'

When answering internal calls, your name, department or extension number are sufficient.

'Susan Madeley speaking' or
'Accounts department' or
'2196'

Don't eat or drink on the phone!

Helpful tips

✔ *Always* have a pen or pencil and paper to hand.
✔ Answer *promptly*.
✔ *Never* eat or drink whilst speaking on the phone.

If the caller wants to speak to someone who *is* available

a find out the caller's name
b ask them to 'hold the line please' *never* 'hang on'
c tell the person requested they are wanted and by whom. (It is a good idea to use the secrecy button – just in case the person requested does not want to speak to the caller at that time!)

If the person requested *is not* available

a ask if you can be of help
b see if they would like to speak to someone else
c give a time when they could ring back or, depending upon company policy, offer to get the person requested to ring them back
d offer to take a message.

✔ Try not to keep callers waiting unnecessarily.
✔ Avoid spending too long speaking to a caller – it can be expensive and time-wasting *and* prevent other people from using the line.
✔ Take care not to give confidential information over the telephone.
✔ *Never* use slang words to callers

'You what?'
'OK'
'See you'.

(How many more slang expressions can you think of?)

✔ Try to use the caller's name during conversation.

'I'm sorry Mr Matthews, Mrs Fenton is not available this morning.'

✔ Always thank the caller for ringing when concluding a call.

Occasionally you will need to deal with callers who have dialled the wrong number or who have been put through to the wrong extension. Don't become impatient. Try to offer help by

- repeating your telephone number so that the caller may check whether they have misdialled
- transferring the caller to the correct extension
- returning the caller to the switchboard to be connected to the correct extension.

Find out how to transfer calls back to your switchboard or to other extensions on your telephone system.

Write down the procedure to help you to remember what to do.

Rules for taking messages

Telephone callers and face-to-face callers will often ask you to pass a **message** on to someone who is not immediately available.

It is important therefore to have the following to hand:

- pen or pencil
- scrap paper for jotting down notes
- message pad on which to write out the messages neatly.

There is no excuse for keeping callers waiting with 'Just let me get a pen,' or 'Wait whilst I find some paper.'

When taking the call

- Ask for the caller's name and company at the beginning of the conversation. You will then be able to use their name during your conversation.
- Ask who the message is for – the caller is not always sure who is dealing with the matter.
- Listen to the message carefully, jotting down important points e.g. figures, names, times, dates.
- Do not attempt to write down *everything* the caller says – it is not necessary!
- Ask for clarification on days – e.g. 'next Wednesday' – find out the exact date.
- Ask for the telephone and extension number of the caller if they want a return call.
- Check important facts by repeating times, dates, names and figures to the caller.
- Use the telephone alphabet to clarify similar sounding names e.g. Mr **P**arker or Mr **B**arker (*see page 64*).
- Write out the message neatly as soon as the caller has left or rung off. It can be forgotten if left!
- Write your message in simple, sentence form. Brief notes are often not clear e.g. 'Will ring'. 'Confirm'.
- Decide whether the message is urgent and therefore needs to be passed on immediately.

Read through these messages.
What is wrong with them?

MEMO

From: The Manager - West End
To: Mr Lincoln   Garage

Message: The figures which
you wanted are as follows:
Van Service £90, Seat
Covers £30 - Making a
total of £120. Can you
let him have a cheque
asap?

Tel no - 374988
Ext no - 2169
Date: 11 March 199_
Message received by: Andrea at
2.30 pm

MESSAGE

For Joan Appleton
From Peter Green
Company Nat West
Date 12 March 199_
Time 9 am
Urgent/non-urgent

Arrive 12 noon. Take
taxi. Will bring
accounts. Ring.

Tel: 0293 482173 x 3174

Taken by Michael

MESSAGE FOR: Peter Stancliffe **FROM:** Sheila Gardner
OF Jones and Clayton
DATE: 10 March 199
TIME:

TELEPHONE CODE 0405   NUMBER 632198   EXT -
TAKEN BY: Louise
MESSAGE

Can you please ring Sheila Gardner
within the next hour?

TELEPHONED ☑   PLEASE RING BACK ☑   RETURNED YOUR CALL ☐   WILL RING BACK ☐   WOULD LIKE TO SEE YOU ☐   URGENT ☑

MEMO

From: Mrs Lucas
To: Mr Lincoln

Message: Mrs Lucas wants
you to phone her about
the estimate which you
gave her for the kitchen.
She will be at her
daughter's house for the
rest of the day. Can you
ring her there?

Date: 8 March 199_
Message received by: Andrea at
10.40 am

MEMO

From: Jade Benton - PKT Ltd
To: Joan Appleton

Message: Can you book
overnight accommodation
(B+B only) for the 4 reps
from London for the
night of 27 March? The
reps' names are Jeremy
Walton, Claire Jenkins and
Simon Scott.

Tel no - 321758
Ext no - 1947
Date: 9 March 199_
Message received by: Andrea at
11 am

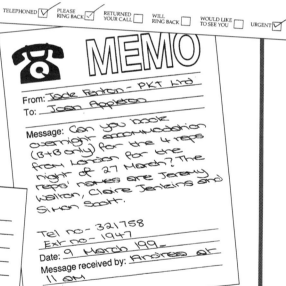

MESSAGE

For Mr Parkinson
From Mr Sinclair
Company Head Office
Date 7 March 199_
Time 3.15 pm
Urgent/non-urgent

The monthly meeting
for next month has
had to be changed.
It will now be on
Thursday.

Taken by Louise

Telephone messages

There are many different types of message pad available such as:

- a pad of blank notes with adhesive strips on the reverse, enabling them to be stuck down to any surface
- a pad of printed telephone message sheets
- a book of tear-out message sheets with NCR duplicate copy to be kept for reference
- scrap paper kept by the phone – cheap but adequate!

Whichever type of message sheet is used, *always* include

- name (and company) of caller
- telephone and extension number
- date and time of call
- details of the message
- the name of the person who has taken the message.

Effective questioning

In order to pass on a complete message, you will often have to ask the caller for more information.

Questions should be asked in a courteous manner and not 'fired' at the caller.

'Who for?'
'How much?'
'What time?'

Abrupt question such as these can give a bad impression.

It can be helpful to the person receiving the message if you can give some indication as to why the caller is telephoning.

Compare these two messages.

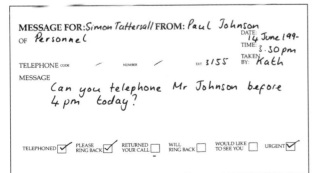
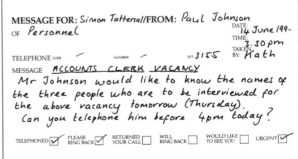

If Mr Tattersall is given the message on the right, he can make sure he has the information requested to hand *before* he returns Mr Johnson's call.

Sometimes callers automatically ask for a person in a senior position because they believe that person is dealing with the matter. By effective questioning, you may discover that the message can easily be dealt with by a secretary, an assistant or even yourself!

Passing on information

- Urgent messages must always be passed on immediately. If the person who should receive the message will not be returning for some time, it is advisable to see if someone else can deal with the message.
- Occasionally, it can be helpful to give some information verbally with your message.

  'Miss Lewis was extremely upset.'

- Always write down messages. Never rely on remembering to tell the person – you will most likely forget!

Making outgoing telephone calls

The secret of making outgoing telephone calls is … *preparation!*

Before making a call, write down

- the full code and number of the company you are calling
- the name of the person to whom you wish to speak
- full details of what you want to say – preferably in logical order.

When you have been connected

- Ask for the person, department or extension number you want.

  'Can I speak to Martin Cooper please?' or
  'Personnel section please' or
  'Can I have extension 2145 please?'

- Be prepared to give your name and the name of your company.
- When your call is transferred, repeat your name and company if necessary and check that you are speaking to the person requested.
- State clearly why you are making the call.
- Tick off the points on your list as they are dealt with.
- Spell out any unusual words. Use the telephone alphabet.

A – Alfred	J – Jack	S – Samuel
B – Benjamin	K – King	T – Tommy
C – Charlie	L – London	U – Uncle
D – David	M – Mary	V – Victor
E – Edward	N – Neville	W – William
F – Frederick	O – Oliver	X – X-ray
G – George	P – Peter	Y – Yellow
H – Harry	Q – Queen	Z – Zebra
I – Isaac	R – Robert	

- Make a written note of important facts.
- Conclude the call by thanking the person for their help.

Practise finding telephone numbers quickly.

You will need a copy of your local telephone directory.

Look up the telephone numbers for the following organisations and services in your area. Write them down to compare with the other members of your group. See who is the first to finish.

1 Town Hall
2 Your local hospital (with Casualty Dept)
3 Nearest international airport
4 Railway timetable enquiries
5 Job Centre
6 Gas Board (to report a gas escape in your area)
7 Social Security Office
8 AA 24-Hour Breakdown Service

Can you find these international codes from your local directory?

9 Dublin, Southern Ireland
10 Tenerife
11 Rome
12 Munich

Did you find all these numbers and codes? Your geographical knowledge may help with the last three!

Confirming telephone arrangements

To avoid misunderstandings or appointments being forgotten, a telephone call is often followed by some form of written confirmation e.g.

● a job appointment confirmed by letter
● an order for goods confirmed by an official order form
● meetings confirmed by letter, memo or fax
● accommodation bookings confirmed by letter, memo or fax.

Answering machines

Telephone answering machines enable callers to leave messages when the telephone is not manned (e.g. lunch times or outside normal working hours).

A tape with a pre-recorded message invites callers to leave a message after a special tone is heard. Later the tape is rewound and the messages played back. The same tape is generally re-used.

Tips for leaving answerphone messages

✔ Begin to speak only *after* the special tone.
✔ Announce clearly who you are (and the name of your company).
✔ State who the message is for.
✔ Spell out any unusual words e.g. names, addresses.
✔ Make the message fairly brief or the tape will run out.
✔ Ring off.

Practise leaving the following messages on an answering machine. (You could use an ordinary tape recorder with a blank tape.)

Assume you work for the Textile Manufacturing Company who are suppliers of soft furnishings to the hotel and restaurant business. Their telephone number is 374653.

Your supervisor, Mrs Meredith, has asked you to telephone the following businesses. She has warned you that most of them will be busy at lunch time and will probably have their answering machines switched on.

Make notes beforehand to ensure that your messages are accurate and clearly delivered.

Message 1 – Kingfisher Restaurant

Tell Mr Saunders that the workshop has finished making the drapes for the two bay windows in the lounge. Two fitters could come over and fix the drapes on Friday of next week. (Make sure you give the correct date.) Ask Mr Saunders to telephone Mrs Meredith as soon as possible to let her know whether morning or afternoon would be more suitable. Be sure to leave our company telephone number.

Message 2 – Planet Hotel

Thank the Manager for his telephone enquiry. Inform him that we can renew linings to existing curtains. Tell him our estimator will be in the area next Monday (give the date). If he would like the estimator to call, ask him to telephone Mrs Meredith and we can arrange a convenient time. Give him our telephone number.

Mention that we are running a special promotion for the next two weeks. We are offering a 25 per cent discount on all dry-cleaning. Our estimator can supply details.

Message 3 – Rooftop Bar

Ask Mrs Templeton to telephone our estimator, John Prescott, to confirm which of the two designs she has chosen for the seating in the restaurant. Remind her that 'Magnolia' is the design with the blue background and 'Petunia' is the multi-floral design. Tell her that the fitters will be able to complete the refurbishment of the restaurant by the end of this month.

Telephone reference books

Your most valuable reference book should be the one compiled by you! A notebook with the telephone numbers of people who you call regularly is easy to refer to. Alternatively, frequently called numbers can be stored in the telephone memory and redialled by just pressing two buttons.

Other directories should include:

- local phone book
- local *Yellow Pages*
- directories for areas called regularly
  (e.g. London, Manchester, Birmingham)
- Thomson's local
- an alphabetical list of the names of people working in your company with their extension numbers.

Telephone services

100	For operator help in making a UK call, 24 hours a day, 7 days a week (free)

150 personal customers **152 business customers**	For information on BT products, services, complaints, phonebook entries or other enquiries	8 am – 6 pm Mon – Sat

151 personal customers **154 business customers**	To report a fault, 24 hours a day, 7 days a week

153	To obtain an international number, 24 hours a day, 7 days a week (There is a charge for this service; however, most international calls can be made direct using IDD service.)
155	For operator help in making an international call, 24 hours a day, 7 days a week (free)
192	For directory enquiries in the UK and Irish Republic 24 hours a day 7 days a week (You will be asked for the name and town. There is a charge for this service.)

Special BT numbers

8081	Accurist timeline (Used to be known as speaking clock.)
Freefone 0800	No charge for using this service (All freefone numbers are prefixed 0800. Companies offer this service to encourage and promote business.)
0345	Information line used by companies – calls are charged at local rate only, no matter where in the country you are phoning from
0891 **0898**	Offers information and entertainment – calls are charged at a higher rate than the standard call rate

Note: Directory enquiries calls are *only* free if

● you cannot use the phone book because of a disability or medical condition
● you are using a public payphone.

Note: From 16th April 1995 (Phoneday), in order to create more telephone codes and numbers, all UK area codes will begin with 01 (instead of 0).

Because of the need for extra capacity, the codes for the following 5 cities will change completely.

Bristol	0117	9	
Leeds	0113	2	
Leicester	0116	2	followed by the 6-digit number
Nottingham	0115	9	
Sheffield	0114	2	

International codes will begin 00 (instead of 010) bringing us into harmony with Europe.

Telephone faults

- Sometimes a bad connection can result in a crossed line, faint volume or line interference. It is better to ring off and try again rather than persevere.
- Whenever a particular number is difficult to obtain, ask the operator (dial 100) to check the line. It is possible that the receiver has not been correctly replaced.
- Report faulty equipment as soon as possible, rather than hope the fault will correct itself.
- BT now prides itself on dealing with most faults on private lines within one working day, and on business lines within five hours!
- To report a fault, private customers should dial 151, business customers 154.

Telephone charge rates

It is important to be aware of the different **call rates** which relate to different times of the day and the day of the week.

- **standard rate**   8 am – 6 pm Monday to Friday
- **cheap rate**   6 pm – 8 am Monday to Friday
  and 6 pm Friday – 8 am Monday (weekend)

Charges vary depending on the distance being called. Distances are given in your local telephone directory under the section on 'Charging information'. BT also issue **charge booklets** for reference.

Remember

Telephone charges depend on

- the **call rate** (standard or cheap or special weekend rate)
- the **distance** being called (local, national or international)
- the **duration** of the call (calculated in units).

For obvious reasons, many business telephone systems bar employees from making international connections.

An itemised print-out of calls can be requested to help keep a check on telephone costs.

Emergencies and security procedures

Confidentiality   *Never* give confidential information over the telephone. You may be overheard by someone listening in on an extension.

Emergencies   Dial 999 for police, fire or ambulance.

- State which service is wanted.
- Give clear details of the emergency (including your name, address and telephone number).
- Answer any other questions clearly e.g. directions to the scene.

Bomb threat   **Don't panic!**

Try to obtain as much information as possible from the caller – time, whereabouts.

Stay calm and *think*. Was the caller drunk? Was it a child? In such cases you would probably consider this a low risk call. However, if it was a mature person – perhaps with a distinctive accent – you should consider this to be a more serious threat. The following is a check list of the actions which should be taken by anyone receiving a threatening call. The list could be kept by the telephone, to be completed by whoever receives the bomb threat. It may assist police to trace the caller as well as locate the bomb!

Check list for use of telephonists

ACTION TO BE TAKEN ON RECEIPT OF A BOMB THREAT

Immediately alert someone else if possible but
DO NOT PUT DOWN THE HANDSET OR CUT OFF THE CALLER.

Obtain as much information as you can.

Try to keep the caller talking (apologise for the bad line, ask him to speak up etc.). Complete this form as you go along, asking questions in sequence as necessary.

Message (*exact words*) _____

_____

_____

Where is it? _____

What time will it go off? _____

What does it look like? _____

What kind of bomb is it (type of explosive)? _____

_____

Why are you doing this? _____

Who are you? Name: _____

Address: _____

_____

Time of call: _____

_____

**When the call has finished give this form to a
supervisor who will decide what to do. The more
information you get, the easier it will be to decide
whether the warning was genuine or not.**

Complete the following as soon as practicable.

DETAILS OF CALLER

MAN ☐   WOMAN ☐   CHILD ☐   OLD ☐   YOUNG ☐   NOT KNOWN ☐

SPEECH

Intoxicated ☐   Irrational ☐   Rambling ☐   Confident ☐

Speech impediment ☐   Laughing ☐   Serious ☐   Hesitant ☐

Nervous ☐   Accent ☐

Was the message Read ☐   Spontaneous ☐

DISTRACTIONS

Any noise on the line? ☐   Call box/pay tone or coins ☐

Car phone ☐   Operator interruptions ☐

Anyone in background ☐

OTHER NOISES

Traffic ☐   Talking ☐   Typing ☐   Machinery ☐

Aircraft ☐   Music ☐   Children ☐

Any other information:

Person receiving call: **Name** _____

Job Title _____

Number of telephone on which call was received

_____

Facsimile transmission (fax)/telex

Fax

Most businesses today possess fax machines. Indeed, they are so useful that they are becoming increasingly popular in the home.

The machine is connected to the telecommunications system, enabling a variety of documents to be sent quickly and easily to any part of the country as well as abroad. Transmissions could include handwritten or typed documents, photographs, diagrams – in fact, anything that can be photocopied.

Although the existing telephone line can be used to receive fax messages, most businesses have a separate fax line (and number) to prevent the line being permanently busy.

Modern fax machines combine telephone, answering machine and photocopier in one streamlined package.

Four essentials in one neat package

Either visit your local telecommunication shop or send away for an up-to-date brochure on fax machines.

Prepare a report to give to your tutor, listing the numerous features offered by fax together with prices to either rent or buy. Incorporate some illustrations of the various models.

Telex

Telex is essentially electronic mail which operates over a public network but has been overtaken in popularity by fax.

Connection to the telecommunications system is necessary.

Messages can either be keyed in direct by the telex operator or, if using a modern personal computer (PC), keyed in and stored, then transmitted (down-loaded) at a convenient time – usually when rates are cheaper.

Electronic mail (E-Mail)

E-mail comprises basically of computer terminals connected to the telecommunications system, enabling messages to be passed between them.

The messages are keyed in (or scanned), then transmitted to other computers via a 'mailbox' system where they are stored, waiting to be read by the receiving user.

E-mail is being used increasingly for **internal** communications by many companies.

New Telecom Gold or New Prestel are the main organisations offering mailbox services for sending E-mail **externally**.

Many businesses have managed to reduce the amount of paper being generated (e.g. memos, letters) by using E-mail to communicate.

Advantages of E-Mail

Messages

✔ are speedier to transmit than using the postal mailing system
✔ can be prepared and sent (down-loaded) after 6 pm when rates are cheaper
✔ can be forwarded to other teminals
✔ can be sent to several mailboxes at the same time
✔ can be accessed by travelling business people using portable laptop computers
✔ can be kept confidential by using a password to prevent unauthorised access.

Note: Internal E-Mail communications are free but **external** communications can be expensive to send.

SECTION REVIEW

Complete the sentences below, using each of the following words *once* only.

TouchTone	message
answering	extensions
Yellow Pages	freefone
secrecy	reference
VDU	standard

1 To prevent callers overhearing your conversations with colleagues, you should press the _____ button.

2 Between 8 am and 6 pm, telelphone calls are charged at _____ rate.

3 A large modern PABX switchboard could be linked to a _____ enabling the operator to view the system at one time.

4 _____ telephones are only available for customers connected to a modernised digital exchange.

5 _____ is an important telephone reference book.

6 An _____ machine is ideal for those people who are not always available to answer the telephone.

7 If the person requested by the caller is unavailable, you should offer to take a _____.

8 On a multiline system, up to 80 _____ can be accommodated.

9 A selection of _____ books should always be kept near the telephone.

10 _____ numbers begin with 0800.

Fill in the missing letters, then write the completed words in your folder to help you remember them.

1 As well as the telephone number, it is advisable to obtain the caller's e___ns__n number so that the call can be returned quickly.

2 If you need to clarify the spelling of a name, use the telephone a_ph_b__.

3 When making appointments, if it is better to obtain the d__ and date to prevent confusion.

4 To obtain sufficient information to pass on a message, you often need to q__s___n the caller.

5 If a message is u_g__t, it should be passed on immediately.

6 When answering the telephone, you should always have a __n or __nc_l to hand.

7 As well as a written message, it is useful to pass on v__b_l information.

8 All messages should be written out clearly and n__tl_.

9 A friendly impression is created if you use the caller's n___ occasionally during a telephone conversation.

10 As well as the date, you should always record the t___ when a message is received.

Wordsearch

Look at the grid shown below and find the following words.

FAULTS

STANDARD

EMERGENCY

CHARGES

CHEAP

OPERATOR

DIRECTORY

INTERNAL

SECURITY

YELLOW PAGES

R	B	O	P	E	R	A	T	O	R	S
D	I	R	E	C	T	O	R	Y	E	Y
J	N	S	G	H	J	I	Y	G	E	C
C	T	R	H	E	J	K	A	Y	S	N
H	E	S	W	A	Z	P	X	N	I	E
A	R	D	G	P	W	F	H	G	A	G
R	N	G	T	O	E	A	W	S	N	R
G	A	L	L	P	I	U	T	E	D	E
E	L	L	A	S	X	L	C	Q	A	M
S	E	C	U	R	I	T	Y	Y	R	E
Y	S	E	Q	S	D	S	G	Y	D	T

5.2 Supply information to meet specified requests

This section covers

▶ information sources
▶ how to use reference books
▶ copyright law

▶ presentation methods
▶ deadlines and targets.

? 'Can you find me the phone number for Heathrow Airport?'
? 'Where can I find the name of a magician for my daughter's birthday party next week?'
? 'Do not type the penultimate paragraph.' What does penultimate mean?
? 'How far is it by road from Cardiff to Liverpool?'
? 'Which motorway will I need to use when travelling from Bristol to Exeter?'

Do you know where to look for the above information?

● Airport telephone numbers are listed at the beginning of all local telephone directories.
● A magician would be listed under 'entertainers' in *Yellow Pages*.
● The meaning of 'penultimate' can be found in a dictionary.
● Mileage distance charts are given in books such as the AA handbook, diaries and road map books.
● Motorways are shown on most UK road maps.

Information sources

Where do you look for information?

● **People who you work with** have a wealth of knowledge about the company, its products and working procedures – acquired from years of experience.
● **Organisations to contact**
  – Citizen's Advice Bureau (CAB) – Department of Social Security – AA and RAC
  – Chamber of Commerce – Inland Revenue – Travel agents
  – Town Hall – Insurance brokers – Banks
  – County Council – Rail companies
● **Royal Mail**
  – **Post Office Counters Ltd** for leaflets on postage services and current postage rates, one-year passports and motor vehicle taxation.
  – **Letter delivery offices** for enquiries regarding deliveries of letters.
  – **Parcelforce** for all types of parcel delivery services.
● **British Telecom** for details of all telecommunication services.
● **Local Reference Library** – to research information from reference books, periodicals and computer databases. Back issues of newspapers are often kept on microfiche. (Photocopying facilities are usually available for a small charge.)
● **Viewdata, New Prestel** – over 250 000 pages of information can be viewed on computer screen. Reservations can be made via the keyboard.
● **Teletext**
  – Ceefax (BBC)
  – Oracle (IBA) } Pages of information can be viewed at home on the television screen.
● **Databanks**
  Many libraries now have computer databanks where a wide variety of information can be accessed by computer.

- **Newspapers** (local and national)
  As well as current news articles, daily temperatures, currency exchange rates and share values are given.
- **Magazines**
  Specialist trade publications, consumer magazines such as *Which?*
- **Telecommunications directories**
  Telephone, *Yellow Pages*, Telex, Fax
- **Reference books**
  - **Dictionary** for spellings, meanings and pronunciation of words. Also includes the meanings of commonly-used abbreviations.
  - **Thesaurus** gives alternative meanings of words
    Pear's Cyclopaedia for information on a variety of topics – published annually
  - *Whitaker's Almanack* a general reference book – published annually
  - **Atlas** for maps and other information
  - **Road maps**, **A–Z street guides** useful for people who travel a lot
  - *Fowler's Modern English Usage* to check points of grammar
  - *Titles and Forms of Address* by Black gives the correct way to address a titled person
  - *Who's Who* published annually gives brief details of famous people. Other publications include *Who Was Who* and *International Who's Who*
  - **AA and RAC handbooks** for details of hotels, UK road maps, main town street maps and other types of motorist information

Ask your tutor to let your look at a business desk diary for the current year. Make a list of all the different types of information contained in the pages at the front. Compare your list with those of others in your group who have looked at different diaries. Did you realise that all this information is so easy to find?

How to use reference books

- Check that the reference book which you are using is up to date.
- Make sure you know how to find information quickly from books. Rather than just flicking through the pages, refer to the contents page listed at the beginning.
- If you can't find the topic you are looking for, it could possibly be listed under another word.
  New **P**restel would be found under **V**iewdata systems
  Tally rolls under **A**dd listing rolls
- When using several reference books, place strips of card between the pages you want to use. It saves time if you have to keep turning back to the same pages.

Copyright law

Just as it is illegal for you to make a copy of your favourite music tape or video, the **Copyright, Designs and Patents Act 1988** states that you must not make photocopies from most published books (unless permission has been given by the author). However, most educational organisations are granted licences, upon payment of a fee, for schools and colleges to make limited copies.

If in doubt, check first!

*See page 95 for details of the **Data Protection Act**.*

Where would you look for the following information?

1 A four-star hotel in Blackpool (two sources)

2 Today's currency exchange rate for the French franc (three sources)

3 Flight availability information to Portugal (two sources)

4 Biographical detais of a well-known MP

5 The meaning of the word 'ambiguous'

6 The distance between two UK towns (three sources)

7 Details of tonight's BBC TV programmes (three sources)

8 Yesterday's temperature in Majorca (two sources)

9 The cost of a provisional driving licence

10 The last guaranteed postal date for posting Christmas parcels to Australia

Presentation methods

To help with your presentation techniques, it would be a good idea to work through Chapter 10, Improving your writing skills, pages 145–157.

When you have found the information, pass it on quickly to the person who requested it. You can do this in several ways.

Oral response

Avoid passing on information verbally unless

- it is wanted immediately
- it is short and uncomplicated
- the person can write it down immediately.

Figures, times and amounts of money should always be passed on in writing to avoid confusion.

Written form

Information can be passed on by a

- note   ● memo   ● letter.

See page 152 for composition of business correspondence.

Graph

Some information is better displayed in graph form.

- Line graphs   ● Histograms   ● Bar charts   ● Pie charts

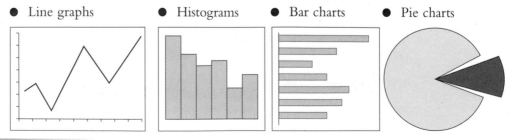

List

Information presented in a list or in table form is clear and easy to follow.

CLIENT TELEPHONE NUMBERS	
R.J. SALISBURY & CO	0764 245663
MASONS TELEVISION REPAIR	0764 278754
THAXTED INSURANCE PURVEYORS	0783 963842
SPIEGELERS OFFICE SUPPLIES	0764 193334
CROMWELL'S AND SONS BUTCHERS	0764 632054
CHERRYTREE OAP HOME	0597 548
BIXLER'S BIKES	0764 654198

COMPANY HOLIDAY ROTA

JAMES	ROGER	ELAIN	JACKIE	SAM
30-5 JANUARY	13-17 JANUARY	27-30 JANUARY	1-5 JANUARY	28-4 APRIL
5-22 JUNE	4-8 MAY	25-29 JUNE	8-18 MARCH	4-9 MAY
2-5 OCTOBER	22-26 JULY	3-8 OCTOBER	2-5 AUGUST	6-10 JULY
9-11 NOVEMBER	2 OCTOBER	1-3 NOVEMBER	23-24 SEPTEMBER	7-11 SEPTEMBER
	12-13 OCTOBER	12-19 NOVEMBER	9-11 NOVEMBER	7-11 DECEMBER
	9-11 NOVEMBER			

Deadlines and targets

When you are asked to find out information

- Try to deal with the request immediately.
- Ask for more details if you are having difficulty finding the information.
- Let the person requesting the information know if there will be a delay e.g. telephone line engaged.
- Try not to get side-tracked by doing another job, or by chatting!
- As soon as you have obtained the information, pass it on immediately in the most suitable form.

'I'll get that information Mrs Pearson wants urgently – as soon as I've put the kettle on and told you about my new boyfriend!'

Complete the sentences below, using each of the following words, *once* only.

Viewdata	deadline
colleagues	graph
directory	newspapers
index	dictionary
microfiche	oral

1 A _____ gives the pronunciation for words as well as the meaning.

2 Fax, telex, and telephone numbers can all be found in the appropriate _____.

3 New Prestel is a _____ system which offers over 250 000 different pages of information.

4 Past issues of newspapers in a reference library are stored on _____.

5 A lot of valuable information can be obtained just by asking _____.

6 Suitable methods of presenting information can include note, memo, letter or _____ response.

7 When using a reference book, look for the topic in either the contents page or the _____.

8 Try to keep to the required _____ when supplying information to senior colleagues.

9 As well as news articles, _____ contain daily temperatures, currency exchange rates and share prices.

10 Visual information is often displayed in _____ form.

Find out the following information from the most appropriate source.

1 The cost of a one-year single passport

2 The telephone code number for inner London

3 The name of the stretch of sea separating the Isle of Wight from the UK mainland

4 What the abbreviation MEP stands for

5 Yesterday's temperature in Miami

6 The price of a weekday edition of *The Times* newspaper

7 The capital of Malta

8 The cost of a road fund licence for a private vehicle for one year

9 The maiden name of Baroness Margaret Thatcher

10 What the abbreviation CV stands for

5.3 Check and process routine, numerical information

This section covers

▶ identifying numerical errors
▶ cross-checking methods
▶ forwarding checked items
▶ reporting procedures to appropriate persons.

Identifying numerical errors

Part of your working day will involve dealing with numerical information such as

● passing on telephone numbers for return calls
● transferring figures from one source to another
● copying numerical lists
● using a calculator to work out answers
● passing on messages involving figures
● adding up or subtracting sums of money
● checking claims for payment
● passing on figures given to you verbally.

Look what can happen if care is not taken when dealing with information involving figures.

Can you identify the errors in the column on the right?

1	Telephone message – ring Jack Simpson on 0772-614328 immediately	*Ring Jack Simpson on 0722 – 614328 immediately*
2	Please let us have your cheque for £1097.64	Please let us have your cheque for £1079.64
3	6296 696 770 43 *Can you total these for me please?*	6296 696 770 43 ‾‾‾‾‾ 21386
4	£27.63 × 3 =	=£8289
5	All orders over £2000 are given a discount of 5%	All orders over £200 are given a discount of 5%
6	6000 -399 ‾‾‾ *Can you insert the answer*	6000 -399 ‾‾‾ 5701
7	*Please calculate for me* Petrol claim 326 miles @ 21p per mile	<u>Petrol claim</u> <u>326 miles @ 21p per mile</u> =£6846
8	Ten thousand and six	1006

Have you spotted all these rather careless errors involving figures?

They include

- transposing numbers (**1** and **2**)
- not aligning figures correctly (**3**)
- not inserting a decimal point when using a calculator (**4**)
- omitting zeros from figures (**5** and **8**)
- incorrect subtraction (**6**)
- not realising 21p should be keyed in as .21 when using a calculator (**7**).

Cross-checking methods

You must take responsibility for ensuring that all calculations made by you are correct. You cannot rely on someone else spotting your errors. Errors which go unnoticed will cause serious inconvenience to your employer and may eventually lead to your dismissal.

Precautions should include

- concentrating when dealing with figures
- using a ruler to avoid returning to the wrong line
- transferring digits in twos e.g. 69 96 84 48
- counting the rows afterwards when typing rows of figures in case one has been omitted
- aligning tens under tens and units under units to assist adding up
- ensuring the correct number of zeros are written for thousands, hundred thousands and millions
- making sure the decimal point is entered when using a calculator – not guessing afterwards!

'This is so much easier than using a calculator, Mrs Pearson!'

Forwarding checked items

The type of documents you are likely to be asked to check are claims for payment. These claims could be

- delivery notes against order forms
- invoices for goods received
- month end statements
- claims for payment from petty cash
- petrol and expense claims from representatives.

Very often more than one person is involved in checking claims for payment to ensure that errors are not missed. The checked document is usually printed with a rubber stamp showing the various checking stages. Each person who has been involved in the checking process initials their appropriate box.

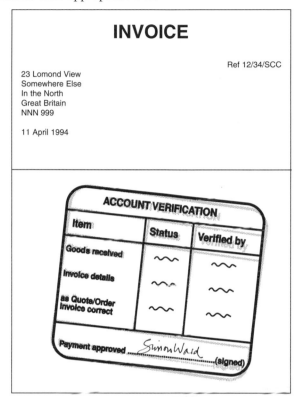

Large computerised businesses which receive hundreds of invoices daily rely upon errors being discovered by inputting the invoice details into the computer which, in turn, should match the initial calculations entered previously from the order form. Any discrepancy will show up at this stage. Smaller businesses may just check the larger invoice amounts (say over £100) and random checks may be made on the remaining invoices.

When checking invoices, follow this procedure.

● If VAT has been added to the invoice, check that the VAT registration number is shown on the invoice
● Check that the invoice is actually addressed to your company, not addressed to someone else and sent to you in error!
● Check for a **valid** order number or the identifying name of the person who ordered the goods – employees could order goods for themselves!
● Check the quantity, description of the goods and price against that on the purchase order.
● Check that the goods have actually been received – have you got a **goods received note** (GRN). Some companies are rather too quick at sending invoices!
● Check that the quantity and description of the goods agrees with that on the GRN. It is possible that only part of an order has been sent!
● Finally, check all calculations for accuracy. Has the discount been taken off and the VAT added on, and not vice versa?

After checking, claims are usually authorised for payment by a senior member of staff.

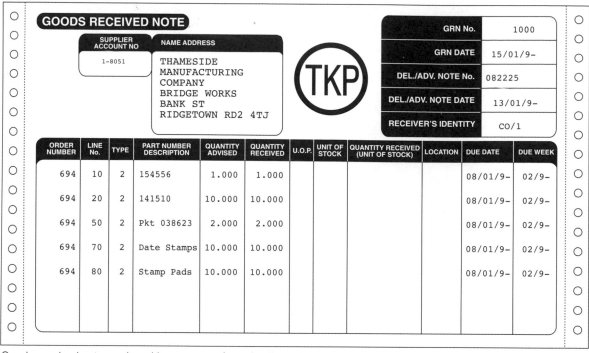

ORDER NUMBER	LINE No.	TYPE	PART NUMBER DESCRIPTION	QUANTITY ADVISED	QUANTITY RECEIVED	U.O.P.	UNIT OF STOCK	QUANTITY RECEIVED (UNIT OF STOCK)	LOCATION	DUE DATE	DUE WEEK
694	10	2	154556	1.000	1.000					08/01/9-	02/9-
694	20	2	141510	10.000	10.000					08/01/9-	02/9-
694	50	2	Pkt 038623	2.000	2.000					08/01/9-	02/9-
694	70	2	Date Stamps	10.000	10.000					08/01/9-	02/9-
694	80	2	Stamp Pads	10.000	10.000					08/01/9-	02/9-

Goods received note produced by computer from details on the delivery note

Reporting procedures to appropriate persons

If, after careful re-checking, an error in numerical calculations is discovered, this should be brought to the attention of your supervisor or a senior person.

Errors in petty cash requests or expense claims are usually corrected and the originator of the claim is notified of the error and the amendments made before payment is issued.

In the case of errors discovered in invoices received from other businesses, the usual procedure is as follows:

- If the description or amount charged differs from the purchase order, check with the Purchasing Department, who will contact the supplier of the goods for verification.
- If the description or quantity differs from what is on the GRN, check with the Stores Department who will turn up the delivery note to check whether they have recorded the details on the GRN correctly.

If the actual delivery note shows that insufficient goods have been delivered
- either the buying company will issue a debit note to the supplier for the amount overcharged
- or a credit note will be requested from the supplier.

- If goods are invoiced but a record cannot be found of receiving them, it is usual to telephone the supplier asking for **proof of delivery** (POD).
- If an error is found in the calculations, the supplier should be contacted immediately. The supplier may
  - request the buyer to alter the invoice in ink and they will make amendments to their copy
  - ask the buyer to destroy the invoice and they will issue a replacement

Calculate the following. Check your answers with your tutor. You may use a calculator.

1 The cost of 12 table lamps @ £31.65 each

2 The cost of 16 square yards of carpet @ £25.99 per square yard

3 25 square yards of carpet @ £31.50 per square yard
23 square yards of underlay @ £4.50 per square yard
£75 extra is charged for fitting.
What is the total cost for laying the carpet?

4 Calculate the value of the following notes and coins.

$$
\begin{array}{rl}
3 & \times \quad £10 \text{ notes} \\
3 & \times \quad £5 \text{ notes} \\
46 & \times \quad £1 \text{ coins} \\
49 & \times \quad 50\text{p coins} \\
7 & \times \quad 20\text{p coins} \\
6 & \times \quad 10\text{p coins} \\
13 & \times \quad 5\text{p coins} \\
4 & \times \quad 2\text{p coins} \\
3 & \times \quad 1\text{p coins}
\end{array}
$$

5 The cost of 20 video recorders @ £426.95 each

6 Calculate the total of the following cheques ready for paying into the bank – £74.63, £23.82, £193.65, £50, £4.70, 95p

7 Sales for January were 21 216
Sales for February were 23 382
Sales for March were 20 619
Sales for April were 24 843
Sales for May were 25 619
Sales for June were 24 384
Sales for July were 26 393
Sales for August were 27 444
Sales for September were 25 240
Sales for October were 23 191
Sales for November were 22 740
Sales for December were 20 721
What is the average number of sales per month?

8 Write out the following, in figures:
● one hundred thousand and thirty-two
● one million, six hundred
● ten thousand and four

9 Total the following – 89p, £1.10, £1.04, £0.32, 10p, 5p

10 Calculate the average age of Claire aged 5, Tom aged 7, Lisa and Paul both aged 9, Simon, Mark and Hanif, all aged 11.

Wordsearch

Look at the grid shown below and find the following words.

ERRORS

NUMERICAL

CALCULATOR

CHECK

RANDOM

TRANSPOSE

CLAIM

DISCREPANCY

ALIGN

INVOICE

W	E	Y	T	G	F	F	R	T	H	B	P
E	W	R	T	I	N	V	O	I	C	E	U
Q	C	A	L	C	U	L	A	T	O	R	B
E	H	R	G	D	X	Z	A	Q	T	N	S
S	E	C	R	A	N	D	O	M	C	R	Z
O	C	S	B	W	P	T	I	B	O	W	C
P	K	A	W	V	B	A	C	R	B	N	L
S	V	L	B	N	L	N	R	C	A	Q	F
N	D	I	S	C	R	E	P	A	N	C	Y
A	R	G	B	Y	T	U	O	V	F	J	M
R	V	N	U	M	E	R	I	C	A	L	K
T	V	B	N	M	H	G	T	R	E	S	W

6 Store and retrieve information using an established storage system

6.1 Store information using an established storage system

This section covers

- documents for filing
- sorting documents
- filing systems
- filing equipment
- safety
- preparing new files
- indexing systems
- cross-referencing
- confidential files
- bulky or completed files
- document retention
- electronic filing.

Why file?

- Up-to-date information can be found *immediately*.
- Queries can be answered quickly and efficiently.
- Time is not wasted searching through piles of unfiled documents.

'I had it in my hand only a minute ago, Mrs Pearson!'

Documents for filing

Make a list of all the various types of documents which you could be asked to file in an office. Can you think of at least *five* different types? Compare your list with those of the other members of your group.

It is important that papers are not filed away before they have been dealt with. To show that documents have been released for filing, a special mark called a **release symbol** is marked on them. A tick, initials or a large 'F' for 'File' could all be used.

Sorting documents

It saves time if documents are pre-sorted before putting them away in the filing cabinets. A useful aid is a **desk sorter** which is made up of a number of heavy 'pages' each labelled with a letter of the alphabet. Papers can then be placed behind each appropriate page.

After sorting, holes are punched in the documents so they can be attached securely inside the files. Make sure that holes are punched squarely by aligning the centre arrow on the punch with the middle of the document *or* by using the alignment guide on the punch. *Never guess!*

Filing systems

Documents are filed away in order so that they can easily be found again. Most organisations use either an **alphabetical** system or a **numerical** system of classification.

Alphabetical

This is the system most widely used because it is easy for people to operate. However, there are several rules to remember:

Names of individuals

1	File under first letter of surname -----------------------	**K**han, Farida
		Parker, Jason
2	Short before long -------------------------------------	Brown before Browne
3	When surname is same, follow first name or initials -----	Thompson, **A**lice
		Thompson, **L**orraine
		Thompson, **W**illiam
4	Initials before full name ------------------------------	Lucas, **B**
		Lucas, **B T**
		Lucas, **Brian**
5	Mac and Mc – all treated as Mac – file before 'M' -------	**McA**dam, A
		MacDowell, A
		Mason, A
6	Ignore apostrophes ---------------------------------	**O**Brien (O'Brien)

Names of organisations

1	Public bodies filed under name or town -----------------	**P**reston County Council
		Social Security, Dept of
2	Ignore the word 'The' ---------------------------------	**C**atering Centre, The
		Pines Hotel, The
3	Saint and St – all treated as Saint	
4	Initials in company names filed at the beginning of section -	**RTL** Engineering plc
		Rathbone & Company
5	Treat numbers as word e.g. 1st Class Paint Company ----	First Class Paint Company

If you are unsure about the alphabetical order of files, check the order of the telephone directory – it is an excellent guide!

Referring to the rules listed above, write out the following names in strict alphabetical order. Put the surname first as shown in the example

Julian McIvor	Robert Black
7-day Service Company	St Thomas' Nursery
Pauline Clark	R Black
The Bread Shop	Paul Adamson
Peter Clarke	Department of the Environment
Greengage Hotel	R Adams & Co Ltd
VDU Sales Ltd	Trevor Green
Vintage Wine Company	Charles Samuel

> **Example**
>
> Adams, R & Co Ltd
> Adamson, Paul

Numerical

A numerical system is very easy to follow but a separate index must be kept of names in alphabetical order. The file number can quickly be found by checking the alphabetical index.

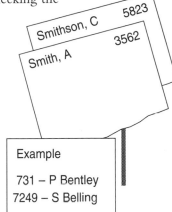

Smithson, C — 5823
Smith, A — 3562

Rearrange the following list into numerical order.
Follow the example shown.

Barker, A	– 74723	Bickley, M	– 77593
Barton, T	– 77472	Bodworth, R	– 76241
Battersby, W	– 75231	Boston, L	– 7621
Belling, S	– 7249	Botham, D	– 7543
Bentley, P	– 731	Bottomly, R	– 77571
Berry, K	– 74256	Burgess, D	– 73814

Example

731 – P Bentley
7249 – S Belling

Take care not to copy figures incorrectly!

There are other filing systems which are sometimes used. These are

- **chronological** – filing by date
- **geographical** – filing by area
- **subject** – filing by topic

Often, documents are filed using two classifications; the main system could be in **alphabetical** order but within each individual file, the documents are filed in **date** order.

Filing equipment

There are *four* main methods of filing documents.

Vertical

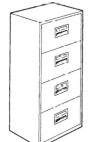

vertical

- Metal cabinets with two, three or four drawers
- Usually files are kept in suspended pockets
- Labels are placed on top of suspended pocket
- Cabinets can be supplied in a variety of colours

suspension filing

Lateral

- Cabinets with shelves with files stored side by side
- Files suspended in pockets
- Labels placed on side of pocket
- Other shelves in cabinet can be used for other types of storage

lateral

Horizontal

- Chest containing shallow drawers for storing plans, photographs
- Labels placed on front of drawer showing contents

Rotary

- Files suspended in pockets on a revolving stand
- Gives all round access
- Labels placed on side of pocket

horizontal

rotary

Safety

! **Never** leave filing cabinet drawers open. People can walk into them. (Modern cabinets will not allow more than one drawer at a time to open.)

! **Always** use a proper filing stool, or steps, to reach high shelves – **never** a swivel chair.

! Cabinets are usually made of metal – this will give documents a limited amount of protection in the event of fire.

! Do not place cabinets too near doors.

Preparing new files

Filed papers are usually kept in a **wallet folder** or can be fastened inside a **manilla folder** to prevent them becoming lost.

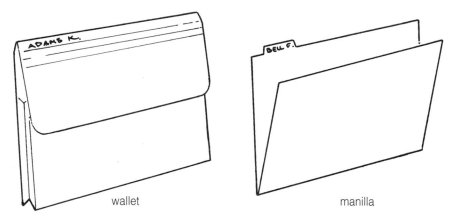

wallet   manilla

A **label** should be attached to the outside of each file clearly showing the title. The label can be typed or boldly handwritten with black pen. The folder is then placed inside the suspended pocket of the filing cabinet.

Your tutor will give you *two* sheets illustrating the shape of files (page 190). Prepare two new files from the details shown below. You could use a stencil, Letraset or perhaps calligraphy writing.

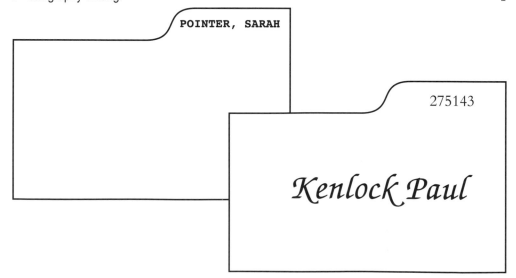

POINTER, SARAH

275143

Kenlock Paul

Indexing systems

Many organisations keep a **card index** of information as well as a file for the topic. As previously mentioned on page 87, an alphabetical index would be necessary to locate files in a numerical system.

Additional information such as address, telephone number and date of birth is often kept on the index card.

Name	JACKSON, IAN J	Number	472
Address	432 CLAREMONT ROAD NORTHAMPTON NN1 1LB		
Telephone No 0604 274318		Date of birth 24-10-65	
Details Previous employment:		Blythe & Co Fenton St Northampton	

Your tutor will give you *four* blank index cards (page 191). Complete each of these with the details given below. They can be either typewritten or handwritten neatly.

STEPHEN FOSTER
27 Canterbury Way
Bristol
BS90 4RG
Telephone 0272 576684
Date of birth 27. 12. 55
Number 3742

HANIF SHAIKH
48 Portland Street
Leicester
LE2 7DD
Telephone 0533 564739
Date of birth 14. 09. 60
Number 2832

PAULINE DIXON
49 Pringle Drive
Dunfermline
KY45 9KJ
Telephone 0383 463532
Date of birth 12. 06. 71
Number 2895

JOHN O'DRISCOLL
312 Devonport Road
Preston
PR5 2FG
Telephone 0772 465832
Date of birth 08. 08. 65
Number 3275

For additional practice, make out an index card for each member of your group. Allocate each member a reference number.

You will need to find out

- full name
- address and post code
- telephone number
- date of birth
- reference number.

Why not collect some additional details of each person such as previous school, hobbies etc, so you can make a note of these on each person's card?

Guillotine each card and practise sorting these into

- alphabetical order
- numerical order
- date of birth order.

Index cards can be stored in a number of ways.

Card index box

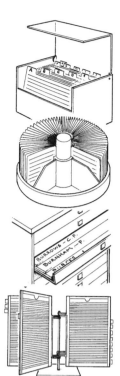

- Cards are filed one behind another, separated by guide cards to assist identification.
- The box can be kept on a desk for quick, easy access.

Rotary index

- Cards are stored in a rotating wheel, enabling the user to see information at a glance.
- Cards can be taken out or added to with ease.

Visible edge index

- Cards are laid out in flat drawers with the title visible at the bottom of the cards.
- Cards can be updated without removing them from the tray.
- Coloured markers on the edge of each card can help identification.

Strip index

- A large book with heavy pages contains strips instead of cards which can be added or removed easily.
- It is only possible to keep a limited amount of information on the strips but different colours can be used to identify topics.

Cross-referencing

Sometimes we look in a telephone directory or *Yellow Pages* for a particular number, only to find that we are directed to look elsewhere.

◆ **Motels**
SEE HOTELS AND INNS

● **Fashion Designers**
See Designers – Garments

◆ **Passport offices**
SEE ALSO POST OFFICES

This redirection is called **cross-referencing**.

Under which letters of the alphabet would you find the telephone numbers for the following?

- National Girobank
- British Gas
- National Blood Transfusion Service
- Job Centre
- Ministry of Pensions and National Insurance
- Royal Naval Establishments

Have you decided?

Now check with the telephone directory. See how you have been directed to the correct place by cross-referencing.

When preparing new files, if a topic could quite easily be filed under two different letters of the alphabet, we could make out a **cross-reference card** which would direct people to the place where the file was actually kept.

> Cross-reference card
> for
> **Time Computing**
> see COMPUTER SUPPLIES

Confidential files

In any company many files contain information which should not be available for others to see. For example in the Personnel Department, files may contain details of medical matters or criminal convictions.

Confidential files should be kept locked in a separate cabinet and only made available to those with the proper authority. They should *never* be left lying on a desk.

Bulky or completed files

Filing cabinets must be inspected at regular intervals – usually between three and six months. If a topic has been completed, the file can be
- taken out but retained elsewhere (often in basement storage), *or*
- destroyed, if no longer required.

Most companies prefer to shred completed files to prevent unauthorised people reading them. Documents are fed into a **shredding machine** which cuts them into unreadable strips.

If a file is still **current** but needs to be thinned out, correspondence that has been in the file for more than a certain period of time (say three months) is taken out and transferred to long term storage.

Current files, however bulky, are *never* destroyed until the matter is completed.

Remember: New files cannot be added to cabinets unless some are first removed!

microfilm

microfiche

An alternative method of storing completed or bulky files is **microfilming**. Important documents are photographed and the negatives are kept in miniature form on either **film** or **fiche**.

A **reader** or **viewer** is needed to view the film or fiche. The images are enlarged and, if a **printer** is also incorporated, a photocopy of the required document can be taken.

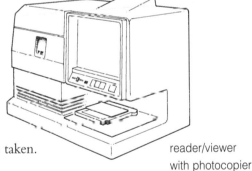

reader/viewer with photocopier

It is possible that you have actually used a microfiche reader or seen one in use. Can you think where?

Document retention

Obviously it is not possible to keep *all* completed files indefinitely and the following guidelines should be observed.

Documents	keep for
Ordinary business correspondence	1 or 2 years
Accounts and VAT documents	Minimum of 6 years (required by law)
Legal documents	minimum of 6 years (important documents should be kept indefinitely)

Electronic filing

Another method of storing information is to input details to a computer.

Instead of preparing handwritten or typed index cards, personal details are keyed into a computer and stored on disk. This method of storage is called a **database** and referred to as **electronic filing**.

The records can be recalled as and when required.

Note: Information stored on disk is often referred to as **data** (hence the word **database**).

Database records

The type of information you may wish to keep in a database could include

- customer records
- student records
- employee records
- library books
- plants stocked by a garden centre.

A typical employee record card would probably look like this.

```
EMPLOYEE  RECORD
SURNAME_____    FIRST NAME_____    M/F __
ADDRESS  _____

         _____
         _____  POSTCODE _____
TEL NO _____    DATE OF BIRTH_____
DEPARTMENT _____    DATE JOINED_____
STARTING SALARY _____   DATE LEFT_____
```

Employee information is keyed into the blank spaces.

These spaces are referred to as **fields** and can be designed to the number of spaces required.

Entering data

A company transferring its employee records from a manual card index to a database system will find that in the initial stages there is a lot of work involved. To input each employee record the database operator will

- bring a blank record to the screen
- key in the employee details to the respective fields
- check that all the entries are accurate – going back and amending any which are not
- finally, save the completed record to disk.

A large database file is generally stored on hard disk rather than floppy disk because of the volume of information.

Once all the manual records have been transferred to the database, the system is easily maintained.

Advantages of electronic filing

In one word – many!

✔ Records can be sorted and printed out in many different ways
    e.g. alphabetical
           gender (male or female)
           department
           age
           joining date
           salary.
           (Print-outs are called **reports**.)
✔ Records are sorted within seconds.
✔ Disk storage space is considerably less than that needed for a manual card system.
✔ Details on each record can easily be updated
    e.g. change of address
           transfer of department.
✔ Records for new employees can easily be added.
✔ Records are quickly deleted for employees who have left.

Amending and updating records

Always

● Check that you are amending the correct record. There may be more than one record for popular names such as John Brown, Alan Jones or Salma Patel.

   Make sure you have selected the correct one by checking the address or age.

● Before storing to disk, double-check that the information you have entered is correct and that *all* relevant fields have been completed.

Note: The amended record is saved in place of the old one.

Your tutor has set up a database for employee records (see suggested record on page 101).

1 Input the employee details shown below. Check that all information on each record is accurate before storing to disk.

2 Upon completion, sort the records into alphabetical order and take a print-out for your file.

3 Select all employees who work in the Sales Department and print out one copy for your file.

4 Three of the employee records need updating. Amend these, save and take a print-out of the three amended records for your file.

   • Kathleen Ford has moved house. Her new address is 5 Appleby Close, Preston, PR4 5FG. Her telephone number is now 642198.
   • Peter Gorse has changed his address to 325 School Lane, Preston, PR4 2DC. His telephone number remains the same.
   • Sarah Eccles has moved from Admin to Accounts.

EMPLOYEE RECORDS TO BE INPUT INTO DATABASE

Name	Address	Tel no	DoB	Department	Date joined	Starting salary
Mr William Slater	50 Clough Road, Preston, PR4 5JK	686432	26.02.48	Sales	14.03.84	£12 900
Mrs Julie Boardman	214 Kent Court, Preston, PR1 3JM	731284	13.11.53	Accounts	21.06.88	£12 000
Miss Pamela Tayor	4 Cornwall Road, Preston, PR2 7KK	432165	21.04.57	Admin	01.09.87	£10 550
Mr Hanif Qureshi	78 Green Lane, Preston PR2 1SX	642139	23.11.70	Admin	11.10.89	£12 650
Mrs Susan Parker	413 Grove Street, Preston, PR3 7MN	325911	13.01.60	Accounts	12.04.87	£9900
Mr Adam Patel	74 Cherry Street, Preston PR2 6GF	553554	27.10.69	Sales	03.02.89	£9500
Miss Kathleen Ford	15 Park Road, Preston, PR3 5FF	742139	01.06.61	Admin	14.12.88	£12 400
Mr Thomas McGuire	321 Rutland Way, Preston PR4 7LP	663844	12.04.70	Sales	15.10.90	£11 350
Mrs Jean Radcliffe	43 Alder Drive, Preston PR2 4DW	342896	12.12.69	Sales	01.08.88	£10 000
Mr David Ryder	3 St Annes Drive, Preston, PR4 2BB	652563	14.09.68	Accounts	12.10.89	£9900
Mr Paul Lambert	15 Hampshire Road, Preston, PR2 9NB	743759	15.10.65	Sales	15.09.89	£10 400
Mrs Jennifer Cooper	435 Branch Road, Preston, PR3 8WQ	663612	12.02.66	Accounts	01.02.87	£14 600
Miss Faroza Lorgat	5 Brindle Way, Preston, PR2 1XC	325981	15.03.73	Accounts	12.11.90	£8250
Mr Gary Jones	50 Lynwood Place, Preston, PR1 5DC	624139	21.12.65	Sales	14.03.89	£9900
Mr Peter Gorse	4 Church Road, Preston, PR3 9TY	553891	03.01.68	Admin	18.07.88	£13 600
Miss Sarah Eccles	58 May Terrace, Preston, PR3 5YT	432817	22.12.67	Admin	22.03.88	£12 200
Mr Carl Haworth	289 Clarence Street, Preston, PR2 5KM	699812	30.12.66	Sales	24.08.89	£14 700
Miss Janet Keen	34 Stanley Street, Preston, PR4 6QA	213312	13.11.71	Admin	22.05.88	£10 500
Mr John Sykes	14 Meadow Road, Preston, PR1 5GB	349614	19.10.63	Accounts	27.04.90	£14 400

Planning and organising work

If one of your duties is to maintain a database

- Try to set aside a regular time each day or week for inputting or amending records.
- Do not let work build up or it will become a mammoth task to clear the backlog.
- Keep records confidential by making sure your VDU screen is not visible to other staff.
- If print-out reports are wanted by colleagues, make sure that you keep to the deadline requested.

'It's all right, Mrs Pearson, I'm just keeping my records confidential!'

Disk copying and back up

Disasters can happen and one of the worst would be if you were unable to access the records in your database because of disk error or damage to a disk.

You must make a habit of copying your work onto a back-up disk each day. If you have stored to hard disk, you will probably need to copy on to more than one floppy disk.

Ideally, the back-up disks should be kept in a separate area from the original in case of fire.

Care of floppy disks

Disks are easily damaged. Look after them by

- writing the label before attaching it to the disk to avoid pressure on sensitive areas
- keeping all disks in dust jackets when they are not being used
- not handling the exposed magnetic areas on 5¼" disks
- storing disks upright in a special disk box and not packing too many in a box
- not letting the disks come into contact with magnetic surfaces or objects as this may wipe off data
- not storing disks near heat or in sunlight.

Prevent anyone accidentally overwriting your disk by

- covering the write protect notch with a tab sticker on 5¼" disks
- moving the protective plastic clip on 3½" disks.

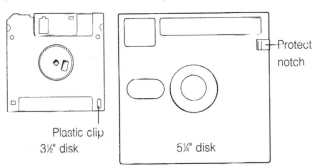

Plastic clip
3½" disk

Protect notch

5¼" disk

Security and confidentiality

A password, only given to certain employees, can prevent unauthorised access to records in a database. The password should be changed frequently.

Note: Passwords do not appear on screen when typed, thus preventing them being seen by other people.

Because many databases contain confidential information, do not leave print-outs lying round. Ensure that discarded print-outs are **shredded** and not just thrown into a waste paper bin.

Do not leave a record on screen for others to see whilst you leave the room.

Information obtained whilst using a database must not be passed on to anyone else.

The **Data Protection Act 1984** states that

- companies holding employee data on computer must register as data users
- information held on computer must be obtained legally
- personal data must not be given to other people
- all data must be kept up to date and be accurate
- companies must ensure that unauthorised access, alteration or destruction is not permitted
- personal records must not be kept any longer than necessary.

Persons are entitled under the Act to

- obtain a list of holders of data by applying to the Data Protection Registrar
- write to the holder of the data requesting a copy of personal information held.

Note: A fee of approximately £1 is charged for this.

Reporting system faults

Sometimes your computer, VDU or keyboard will not work.

Before sending for help, make the following checks on the equipment.

- Is the power switched on?
- Is everything plugged in properly?
- Have you switched the machine on?
- Is the connection between the computer and the VDU secure?
- Has anyone turned the brightness down on the VDU screen, resulting in a blank screen?
- Is the connection between the computer and the keyboard secure?
- Have you inserted a disk in the disk drive?
- Is the disk inserted the correct way round?
- Remove the disks, switch off, leave for 30 seconds, then try again
- Refer to the computer manual.

If you are still unable to discover the fault, you will have to ask for help. Try to be specific about the exact problem you are experiencing. Do not just say, 'It won't work!'

SECTION REVIEW

Can you identify the illustrations shown below? Choose from the list on the left of the page.

- File labels
- Punch
- Stapler
- Box file
- Ring binder
- Card index box
- Vertical cabinet
- Suspension filing
- Filing stool
- Wallet folder

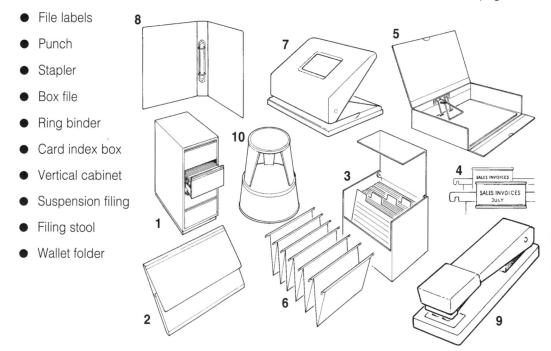

Fill in the blank spaces in the following passage using each of the listed words *once* only.

suspended	vertical
alphabetical	numerical
confidential	index
release	cross-reference
microfiche	sorted

A _____ symbol is marked on all documents which are ready for filing. Before attempting to file documents, they should be _____ into some type of classification, usually _____ or _____. An _____ is always needed when using a numerical classification.

The most popular type of filing system is the _____ cabinet which consists of two, three or four drawers and files are usually kept in _____ pockets.

If a file could be placed under two letters of the alphabet, a _____ card should be made out.

Files which should only be seen by a limited number of people are referred to as _____ files.

To save space, important documents can be photographed and the negatives stored on _____.

Fill in the missing letters, then write the words in your folder to help you remember them.

1 An electronic system of filing record cards is called a _a_a_a_e.

2 The spaces for completing information on a record card are called f___ds.

3 Information kept in a database can be s_r__d quickly.

4 A print-out of database records is called a r_p_rt.

5 To prevent losing work which has been stored to disk a __ck-_p copy should always be made.

6 A _ss__rd will prevent unauthorised persons from accessing your database.

7 Under the __t_ ___t_ct__n Act, employees can request a copy of personal information kept on a database.

8 Disks stored near h___ may become damaged.

9 If your computer will not work, you must first check all __nn_c_io__.

10 Covering the write protect notch on 5¼" disks will prevent anyone from ov__w__t__g your files.

Wordsearch

Look at the grid shown below and find the following words.

ELECTRONIC

RECORD

DATABASE

PRINTOUT

REPORT

DISK

BACKUP

FAULTS

VDU

PASSWORD

E	X	E	O	Y	U	P	T	L	W	N
B	L	K	H	M	Q	L	T	J	K	P
W	V	E	D	F	T	U	U	V	D	U
A	C	H	C	O	O	E	T	E	I	K
F	A	U	L	T	S	Z	U	P	S	C
W	Q	P	N	J	R	D	F	G	K	A
E	R	I	R	E	P	O	R	T	O	B
H	R	E	C	O	R	D	N	N	E	W
P	A	S	S	W	O	R	D	I	P	R
V	B	W	R	H	J	I	R	E	C	Q
V	L	Y	D	A	T	A	B	A	S	E

6.2 Obtain information from an established storage system

This section covers

▶ organisation of filing
  – centralised
  – departmental
▶ locating files

▶ booking in and out procedures
▶ delays in supplying files
▶ reminder systems and overdue files.

Organisation of filing

There are *two* main methods of organising files.

Centralised filing

All the company's filing is kept in one large area.

Advantages	Disadvantages
✔ Filing staff are competent and well-trained.	✗ Files are not always close to hand.
✔ Only one type of classification is used e.g. alphabetical, numerical.	✗ Delays can occur when answering telephone queries.
✔ Missing files are chased up regularly.	
✔ Cabinets and files are maintained in good order.	

Departmental filing

Each department has its own filing system within that department.

Advantages	Disadvantages
✔ Files can be referred to quickly.	✗ Departments may not use the same method of classification throughout the company.
	✗ More cabinets will be needed.
	✗ Staff may not be as competent at filing if other duties need to be done.

Organisations which operate a centralised system of filing often encourage individual departments to keep their own card index record for the people with whom they usually deal.

Can you think why this is so?
What sort of details would you suggest should be kept on each index card?

Locating files

Individual files often need to be taken from the filing cabinet, usually when further information on a particular topic is required.

This could be caused by

● a letter received containing an enquiry
● a personal caller to the office

● a telephone enquiry
● a reminder in the diary.

Because files are continually needed for reference by various people, the following rules must be observed.

- All documents relating to the topic must be filed away regularly – daily, if possible.
- Individual documents or letters must *not* be taken out of a file – a photocopy of the item should be made instead.
- If a file needs to be borrowed, a note in the form of an absent card must be completed and placed where the file is usually kept.
- Files which have been borrowed for more than several days must be chased up and returned.

'Mrs Pearson – your time is up.
You've had that file fo[r]
three days now'

The absent card is put in the place of the borrowed file.

Booking in and out procedures

How many times have you looked in a cabinet for a file only to find that someone else has borrowed it? If you know the name of the person who has taken the file, then there is no problem.

A sensible filing clerk will make sure that no file is taken without an **absent** (*or* **out**) **card** being completed and placed where the file is usually kept. The absent card is completed with details of the file borrowed, name of borrower and date.

When the file is returned to the cabinet, the absent card is removed.

The filing drawers should be checked daily and files which have been borrowed and not returned within a reasonable period of time should be chased up for return.

Your tutor will give you an absent card (page 193). Complete this with the following details of files borrowed.

Cross through each entry if the file has been returned before moving on to the next.

1 Control Services plc file was borrowed on 3 February by Jane Mortimer of Accounts, She returned the file on 5 February.

2 Fatima Sidat of Purchasing took the file for Hamiliton & Co on 7 February and returned it the same day.

3 On 9 February, the file for Key Business Systems was borrowed by Julie Carter of the Technical Department. She returned the file four days later.

4 The file for Mehmood Kahn was borrowed by Gary Rogers of Personnel on 15 February and returned the day after.

5 Tony Wilkins of Sales took the file for Star Engineering plc on 21 February. The file has not yet been returned.

Delays in supplying files

Unfortunately, it is not always possible to supply a file immediately to the person requesting it.

Can you think of *three* reasons for this?

The delay could be because
- someone else is using the file
- the file is currently being updated
- the file has been put back in the wrong place!

Assume that your manager, Robert Kingsley, has requested a file for Mrs Janice Worden. An absent card informs you that this file was borrowed by Simon Boston from Accounts two days ago.

Write down exactly how you would explain to Mr Kingsley why you cannot let him have the file immediately and then state what action you will be taking to obtain the file for him.

Reminder systems and overdue files

Smaller offices will find that checking the absent or out cards in the cabinet drawers periodically is sufficient to check whether files have been borrowed for an unreasonable length of time.

Larger organisations may

- keep a **returns diary** with the files listed under the **date of return**. Files will be crossed out when returned, leaving overdue files to be chased up.

RETURNS DIARY	
DATE OF RETURN	FILE NAME
17/6/9-	Johnson & Co
17/6/9-	~~LONDON STEEL LTD.~~
18/6/9-	~~Billingham Traders Ltd~~
18/6/9-	Emersley Fabrics
18/6/9-	~~MICROMART LTD~~

- make out a card for each file borrowed and file it in a **card index box** under the **date of return**. The card is removed when the file is returned, leaving cards for outstanding files remaining in the box.

RETURN BY	FILE NAME
21/6/9-	NIGHTINGALE LTD

RETURN BY	FILE NAME
18/6/9-	EMERSLEY FABRICS

RETURN BY	FILE NAME
17/6/9-	Johnson & Co

For electronic filing, see page 00.

Fill in the missing letters and then write the completed words in your folder to help you remember them.

1 To ensure that holes are punched squarely, use the _l_gn___t guide on the punch.

2 A numerical filing system needs an __ph_b_____l index.

3 Two types of folder for holding documents are called __ll_t and m___lla.

4 It is usual to have s__p__s___ filing in vertical and lateral cabinets.

5 Where a file could be put in two different places, a ___ss-r__er__ce card should be used.

6 C__f_d__t___ files should never be left lying on a desk.

7 Depending upon the size of the organisation, filing may be centralised or __p__rt__nt__.

8 To indicate that a file has been borrowed, it is usual to complete an _u_ or __s__t card.

9 A r_m__d__ system should be kept to ensure that borrowed files are chased up.

10 As a __fe_y precaution, cabinets are made of metal

Crossword

Across

3 A type of classification (9)

5 Is used before putting documents into filing cabinets (4) (6)

8 A type of filing cabinet (7)

9 A type of file which is retained indefinitely (5)

11 Files are kept in one place (11)

12 A file which has not been returned (7)

Down

1 Is required with a numerical classification (5)

2 A type of filing classification (4)

4 Must be done if a file is not returned (5) (2)

6 Mark to indicate that documents can be filed (7)

7 How often should filing be done? (5)

10 To destroy completed files (5)

Produce text following instructions

7.1 Produce text using a keyboard

This section covers

▶ keyboard equipment
▶ printers
▶ technique and posture
▶ proof-reading documents
▶ checking techniques
▶ correction of errors
▶ styles of layout
▶ sources of information
▶ saving and printing data.

If you have the opportunity of learning to type, it is well worth the time and effort.

Keyboarding accounts for a large proportion of clerical jobs today, from copy typist to secretary and sales assistant to stock control clerk.

Can you think of *oix* different types of job which involve using a keyboard during some part of the day?

Keyboard equipment

Manual typewriter

Not used a lot these days! Plenty of effort is needed to strike the keys – and return the carriage.

manual
typewriter

Electric typewriter

A power supply helps make pressing the keys and using repeat keys far easier.

Electronic typewriter

electronic
typewriter

A reduction in price during the last few years has enabled even the smallest of offices to replace their manuals and electrics with these multi-functional machines.

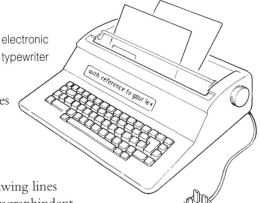

Facilities include

- word wrap-around
- text emboldening
- automatic centring of words
- choice of pitch (size of type)
- justification
- drawing lines
- paragraphindent
- easy correction of errors
- storage of paragraphs into memory
- small display screen.

Word processor

This has an electronic keyboard with VDU (visual display unit) with all the facilities of an electronic typewriter. A word processor allows you to key work into the computer, then save it to disk. Your work can then be recalled from disk at any time. Keyed-in text can be printed out on an attached or shared printer.

Additional facilities include

● easy insertion and deletion of text
● moving and copying text
● mail merge
● spelling check
● word search (to replace or amend)

Microcomputers

Whereas word processors are dedicated to keying-in and recalling text, microcomputers can run a wide range of software, in addition to word processing. This software could include databases, spreadsheets, accounts and desk top publishing programs. (Integrated packages allow the user to run a combination of the afore-mentioned programs.)

Printers

There is a wide selection of printers now available on the market.

● **Dot matrix printers** are the least expensive. Later models can produce near letter quality print (NLQ). Print is formed by a series of dots making up each character.

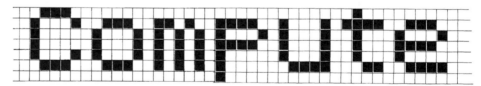

A series of dots makes up each character.

● **Daisy wheel printers** have characters positioned on spokes from a wheel which rotates whilst printing.

● **Ink jet printers** produce high quality copies by squirting small jets of ink onto the paper. They are expensive to buy and the ink cartridge needs replacing periodically.

● **Laser printers** are very fast and print good quality work (including diagrams and pictures). Although they are still expensive to buy, they have come down in price in recent years. The toner cartridge will need replacing regularly and this can also be an expensive item.

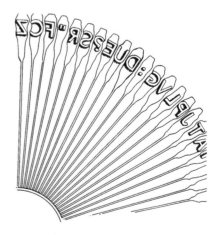

A daisy wheel – one character appears on each 'petal'

Technique and posture

Whichever type of keyboard is being used, ensure that

- fingers remain in contact with the home keys
- shoulders are relaxed – not tense
- arms and elbows hang loose – not stuck out!
- adjustable back rest supports the back
- wrists are level with the keyboard – not resting on it!
- feet are flat on the floor – not dangling in mid-air.

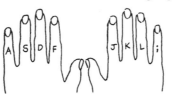

Touch typists have an advantage over those using two index fingers for the 'hunt and peck' method!

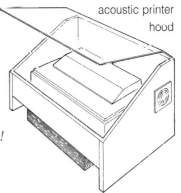

acoustic printer hood

Particularly when using VDUs, remember that

- blinds and curtains will prevent screen glare
- acoustic printer hoods can reduce printing noise
- regular breaks will help prevent eye strain
- if you need to wear glasses for close work – *wear them!*

Proof-reading documents

Get into the habit of always proof-reading each page of your work carefully before taking your paper from the typewriter or storing your work to disk. Errors are far easier to correct whilst your work is still aligned in your machine. It is easier to correct errors as soon as you see them – they can be forgotten if left until later. Make use of the spell check facility on your word processor or computer.

When proof-reading your finished work, follow this procedure.

- Read through each page, keeping an eye on the original document which you have copied from, making sure you have not missed out any complete lines or even full paragraphs.
- Go through your work for a second time, reading **one word at a time**, checking for spelling and typing errors.
- Use a ruler to follow each line, particularly when checking figures.
- If you are doubtful about the spelling of a word, check with a dictionary.
- When checking important documents, ask a colleague to check your work whilst you read aloud from the original document.
- Mark all errors in pencil and also put a mark in the margin so you can correct these immediately.

Remember: Nothing is more embarrassing than having someone point out your errors and, worse still, you having to repeat the work!

See if you can find *one* spelling error and *one* punctuation error in *each* of the following sentences.

1 The commitee will make a decision in one weeks time.

2 Special items of mail should be kept seperate from franked mail?

3 Many items of stock can be ordered from catologues and this method is used by many companies

4 Accomodation in Venice Rome, Florence and Milan was arranged by the travel company.

5 Can you name two occassions when it would not be suitable to wear jeans.

Checking techniques

When typing up documents from manuscript, be on the lookout for obvious errors such as the following:

- … visit you on Thursday, 24 May – *shouldn't this be Thursday, **25** May?*
- … the amount owing is £207.95 (£234 + VAT @ 17½ %) – *shouldn't this be **£274.95**?*
- … confirm our reservation for five nights, 16–19 July inclusive – *shouldn't this be **four** nights?*
- … and whilst I am in Lancashire, I hope to visit Altrincham – *isn't Altrincham in **Cheshire**?*
- … the Company are sure you will understand – *shouldn't this be 'the Company **is** sure'?*

Can you find *five* errors in each of the following paragraphs?

1 Michael was looking forward very much to his first day at Collage has he knew the qual-ificaions which he had achieved would help him to progress atwork.

2 If most ofyour money is in a building society, A fall in intrest rates can only mean a drop on your standard of living

3 Most children watch television for atleast four hours each day? It as been sugested that this is the reason for the fall in reading standard.

4 The heaviest snowfall usually occurs in Febuary although heavy fall have been known to occur in march. I can remember a particularly bad year when i was a child.

Have you found them all?

Use a calculator to check the following.

Make a note of those which are incorrect.

1   There were 47 items priced at £4.95 each, making a total of £323.65.

2   The suite is £1015.79 (£864.50 + VAT @ 17½%)

3   The price of the goods is £1003.80, payable by 12 equal monthly instalments of £83.65.

4   Your deposit of 20% has been deducted from the purchase price of £235, leaving a balance owing of £88.

5   If the balance of £750 is paid within 7 days, a discount of 5%, amounting to £37, can be deducted.

Correction of errors

Manual typewriter

Use liquid paper, applied thinly and allowed to dry completely before overtyping.

Electric typewriter

A correction ribbon is usually incorporated – otherwise use liquid paper.

Electronic typewriter

All have their own correcting ribbons – avoid using liquid paper as this will spoil the daisy wheel.

Word processor or microcomputer

So easy – either use delete keys or just type over errors!

Find a piece of typed work, containing errors, which you have completed earlier.
(It could be a practice typing examination paper.)

Erase your errors by applying liquid correcting fluid, allow it to dry thoroughly and see if you can align your work into the typewriter to make the necessary corrections.

Line your work up vertically first of all using the printing guide on the alignment scale. Then align your work horizontally using the variable interliner.

Styles of layout

Whichever method of document layout you have been taught, you will be expected to follow the style preferred by the organisation for whom you work.

Letter layout

Compare the style of layout of the three letters illustrated below.

A *Fully-blocked letter with open punctuation*

CENTRAL
ENTERPRISES
Falcon Street, Rugby, RG2 4PL

Ref   FH/TL

12 August 199_

Mrs J Scott
33 Clifton Drive
RUGBY
RG1 8GF

Dear Mrs Scott

Thank you for your letter dated 9 August enclosing the information about your investments.

I shall be pleased if you could call to see me on Monday, 19 August at 2.30 pm when I hope to be able to give you the remaining quotations.

Please telephone my secretary if this date is not convenient and arrange an alternative time.

Yours sincerely

F. Hargreaves

FRANCES HARGREAVES
Finance Manager

B *Fully-blocked letter with punctuation*

Backhouse & Company
• Solicitors •
3 Hilton Road • Chester • CH2 5WD

Our ref.   T5678

25th June 199_

The Manager,
Templeton & Co. Ltd.,
Station Road,
CHESTER.
CH1 3GB

Dear Sir,

James Crabtree

The above-named has applied to us for the position of despatch clerk.

Your name has been given as a referee and we shall be grateful if you will give us your opinion, in confidence, as to whether he would be suitable for a position with us. We enclose a job description for the post.

We enclose a stamped addressed envelope for your reply.

Yours faithfully,
BACKHOUSE & COMPANY,

Paul Preston

PAUL J. PRESTON.
Partner.

Enc.

W. H. LYNN & CO.
INSURANCE BROKERS
6 High Street • Carlisle • CR1 4KK

Our ref. WF/KP   22nd May 199_

CONFIDENTIAL

Mr. W. T. Barnes,
67 Bridlington Road,
CARLISLE.
CR1 3GB

Dear Sir,

Southern & Ashworth

The recent insurance claim which you submitted has been forwarded to the above company. They have, however, asked for more information to be supplied by you as to how the fire started.

Will you please complete the enclosed questionnaire and return it to us as soon as possible?

Yours faithfully,
W. H. LYNN & CO.

S. King

SUSAN J. KING
Claims Manager.

Enc.

C *Semi-blocked letter with punctuation*

Note: A is the style favoured by most offices today.

Memo layout

Different companies have their own style of memo design.

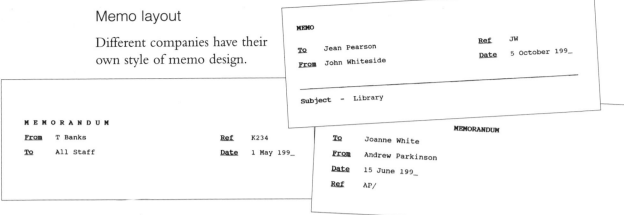

Document numbering

Page numbers can go at the top or bottom of the page, in the centre, or to one side.

Whichever numbering layout is used, be consistent. Keep to the same style for each page.

Note: The first page of a document is not numbered.

See page 116, collating and fastening equipment

Sources of information

When typing documents, there will be times when you need to query parts of the manuscript.

You *must*
- check with the author of the document, *or*
- use a spell check, *or*
- refer to an appropriate reference source
  e.g. spelling   – dictionary
        date   – diary/calendar
        post code – post code directory.

Never guess!

Saving and printing data

Before saving work to disk, you should
- Proof-read your screen very carefully for errors – if you find this difficult, print a draft copy and check this.
- Make sure that your document is paginated sensibly – no single words or final items of a list separated from the remaining text.
- Use the spell check if your spelling is not good.
- Make a note of the name of your document and the disk to which you are saving.

Before printing
- Check that your paper is lined up straight in the printer.
- Take care to print out the correct document – it is a waste of time to select the wrong one!
- Find out how to stop the printer quickly in the event of an emergency.
- Always leave the paper in the printer correctly aligned ready for the next person to use.

SECTION REVIEW

Rewrite or type the following sentences correctly.

1 Correction sign's should always be marked with a different colored pen.

2 Errors could be in punctuation, spelling grammer or layout.

3 all numerical data should be checked for accuracy and any errors or ommisions identified.

4 It is preferably that two people check a document– one reading and the other checking.

5 Errors should be brought to the attention of the author and amendment if neccesary.

6 The Image of the company can be spoiled by badly presented documents

7 If your spelling is pooor, you should use the spell check onyour word proccessor.

8 When typing documents, al-ways read through for error's before taking the page from your typewriter.

9 A dictionery shouldbe used if your spelling is not to good.

10 It is sensible to use a Ruler when checking documents contain-ing figures?

Wordsearch

Look at the grid below and find the following words.

TECHNIQUE

SPELLCHECK

CORRECT

LAYOUT

PRINTER

VDU

ELECTRONIC

DICTIONARY

ACOUSTIC

KEYBOARD

T	F	F	J	Z	W	I	R	M	Z	Y	K
C	S	X	P	R	I	N	T	E	R	C	C
E	J	T	K	E	Y	B	O	A	R	D	E
R	L	E	U	M	X	A	N	H	G	L	H
R	A	E	S	A	C	O	U	S	T	I	C
O	P	U	C	F	I	S	Q	D	U	M	L
C	A	Z	G	T	J	G	U	K	O	L	L
R	W	D	C	C	R	X	G	H	Y	L	E
F	D	I	A	V	G	O	C	L	A	K	P
V	D	U	Y	D	R	B	N	G	L	G	S
F	H	R	T	E	C	H	N	I	Q	U	E
S	Q	S	G	J	O	L	M	T	C	R	S

7.2 Produce copies using reprographic equipment

This section covers

- ▶ methods of reprography
  - – duplicating
  - – copying
- ▶ more information on photocopiers
  - – functions
  - – equipment problems
  - – routine maintenance
  - – improving quality
  - – reducing wastage

- ▶ multi-page documents
- ▶ collating and fastening equipment
- ▶ returning finished work/deadlines
- ▶ confidentiality
- ▶ copyright law
- ▶ ordering and storage of materials.

During the course of each day, many different types of documents have to be copied. This is called **reprography** – making copies.

Methods of reprography

There are a number of ways to do this.

Duplicating

Spirit copier

Used – more in schools than offices

Quality – not very good

Materials – typed or handwritten master copy, liquid spirit (highly flammable!), semi-absorbent duplicating paper

Cost – paper, spirit and master are reasonably cheap.

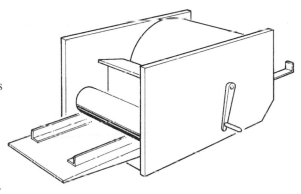

Spirit duplicator

Ink duplicator

Used – in schools, colleges and organisations who need to send out newsletters/information sheets

Quality – reasonably good

Materials – waxed master stencil can be typed or an original is copied onto a stencil by means of an electronic scanning machine, duplicating ink, semi-absorbent duplicating paper

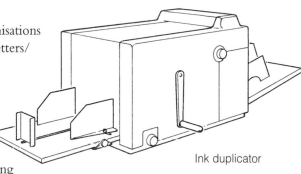

Ink duplicator

Cost – paper, ink and masters are relatively cheap, although the initial purchase of the scanning machine and ink duplicator needs to be taken into consideration. The stencils can be stored and used again.

Offset litho

Used – by any organisation wanting to make numerous copies

Quality – excellent and can print in more than one colour

Materials – paper or metal plates, photocopier needed to copy paper masters, solution for cleaning down machinery after use, good quality copy paper, a trained operator is needed

Offset litho

Cost – the actual duplicating process, for long runs, is reasonably cheap although the offset machinery is expensive to purchase and the training of an operator needs to be considered. The stencils can be used again

Copying

Photocopier

Used – almost everywhere! Many firms have more than one copier

Quality – excellent – sometimes better than the original document

Materials – toner ink (either in cartridge or loose powder), plain paper

Cost – most copiers are rented, charge will include engineer call out. Toner is usually included in the rental fee but paper must be provided by the user. Can prove expensive for long runs – offset would be more economical.

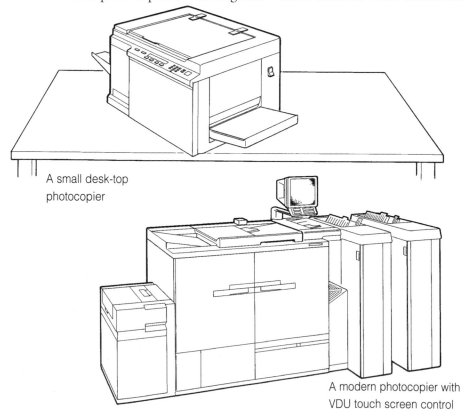

A small desk-top photocopier

A modern photocopier with VDU touch screen control

Three companies rent photocopiers from separate suppliers at different rental rates.

Calculate the total photocopying cost to each company per month. (Paper is bought in packets of 500 sheets.)

Company A

Rental is £35 per month
Paper costs £5 per packet
5000 copies are made each month at a cost of 2p per copy.

Company B

Rental is £50 per month
Paper costs £4 per packet
10 000 copies are made each month at 1.5p per copy

Company C

Rental is £60 per month
Paper costs £3.50 per packet
15 000 copies are made each month at 1p per copy.

Note: When a **microcomputer** has been used to prepare work, if only a few copies are required, it is often quicker and more convenient to print out multiple copies on a computer printer.

More information on photocopiers

Functions

Photocopiers are available in a variety of sizes. The larger models could include all or most of the following functions:

- documents can be fed in automatically
- print quickly
- accept various sizes of paper
- continuous computer print-outs can be copied automatically without the need for separation.
- can copy onto card, labels, offset paper plates and OHP transparencies
- adjustable density control to take account of very light or dark originals
- can enlarge or reduce, with a choice of sizes available
- will copy a document onto both sides of the paper (known as **back-to-back** or **double-sided**)
- stack multi-page documents into separate trays (to assist collating)
- operator can interrupt a job, and then resume

- an additional paper tray
- can staple multi-page documents
- book mode – will photocopy an open book without adjusting the position
- advanced machines can print in colour
- a password number can be keyed in to record the user and the number of copies being made by them. A limit can be imposed.
- larger models can incorporate a VDU for touch screen operator control.
- can store several frequently used copying operations
- can be set to switch on automatically at a set time each day
- edit image – can erase designated areas
- edit image overlay – two original copies can be overlaid into one.

Check the functions available on the photocopier used in your building.

Complete as much as possible of the grid below.

If possible, obtain details of the cost involved

Function	tick ✔
Automatic paper feed	
Photocopy onto card or labels	
Reduce	
Enlarge	
Automatic back-to-back	
Prepare OHPs and offset masters	
Take paper sizes other than A4	
Automatic density adjustment	
Additional paper tray	
Interrupt facility	
Photocopy continuous computer paper	
Book mode copy facility	
Collate documents	
Staple multi-page documents	
Copy in colour (other than black)	
Rental cost each period e.g. quarterly	£
Maintenance fee for each period	
Cost of copy paper per packet	£
Additional charge per copy (if any)	p

Equipment problems

Sometimes, your photocopier will develop faults. Learn how to identify the signals from your copier. Many of these problems can be remedied by you.

The fault signals are common to most makes of machine and the instruction manual will explain these to you. On modern machines, an electronic display panel or VDU gives step-by-step instructions to remedy the fault.

 Personal counter – key to operate the machine has been inserted incorrectly.

 Paper cassette is empty – needs refilling.

 Paper jam – open front cover to remove jammed paper. Electronic display panel will indicate location of jammed paper.

 Toner required – either insert a new toner cartridge or fill with toner powder.

 Used toner container needs emptying – remove container and replace with empty container.

 Developer required – developer replacement should only be carried out by engineer.

 Collator trays need emptying – they have reached the limit which they can hold.

 Service required – call the service engineer as soon as possible. Many engineers can be contacted quickly on their mobile telephones.

Routine maintenance

- Keep the glass clean. Use a special spray.
- Avoid scratching the glass with paper clips or other sharp objects.
- Copiers should not be placed flat against a wall. Air should be allowed to circulate.
- Keep coffee cups and other drinks away from the copier.
- Do not poke inside the copier – send for the engineer if the fault is not easily identifiable.

Improving quality

To make sure that your finished copies are of the best possible quality
- Clean any dirty marks from the document to be copied – a special photocopy correction fluid is more suitable than liquid paper.
- Make sure the glass plate is spotless.
- Place document to be copied face down on plate (if not using automatic feed).
- Line up the document within the correct guide mark sizes – not crooked!
- Adjust the density control according to whether the document is too light or too dark. Lighten the density if you are copying from coloured paper (some copiers will do this automatically).
- Some copiers do not copy pencil or blue ink as well as black ink.
- When copying small pieces, such as newspaper cuttings, place a sheet of A4 behind your cutting.
- Do not use too much adhesive or Sellotape when sticking cut-outs.
- Apply *gentle* pressure to the photocopier lid when copying from thick books, to avoid light getting in.

Reducing wastage

- Check that the previous user has not left the copier set for A3, enlargement, reduction or worse still, 100 copies!
- If A5 size is required, take two copies and place both side by side on A4 paper – only half the number of copies need then be made.
- Make sure your document is placed face down – not facing upwards.
- Take the exact number of copies required – no extras 'just in case'.
- Discourage personal use of the copier by members of staff.
- When refilling the paper tray, make sure the paper is fanned to avoid multi-sheets being fed through.
- *Always* take one test copy to check before making multi-copies.
- Finally, if you are unsure of how to use any functions on your machine – *ask* – it can prove expensive to experiment.

Multi-page documents

- Try to make sure each page is consistently numbered at either the top or the bottom.
- Photocopy pages in their correct order – take extra care with back-to-back pages.
- Always straighten copies squarely by tapping them on the desk top.
- If a collator is not available on your copier, stack each set of pages offset against the previous set.

The copies are then ready for stapling or binding as required.

stacking collated
copy documents

Collating and fastening equipment

Multi-page document can be sorted into the final order by

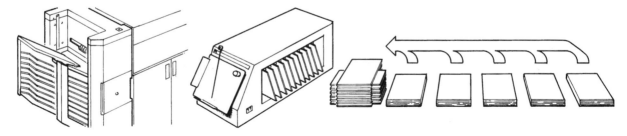

a collator attached to a photocopier   a free-standing electric collator   sorting by hand.

Be sure to check that the first collated pages out of a collator are in the correct order and there are none missing! Make random checks when collating large numbers.

The documents can then be fastened by a number of methods.

- **Stapling** – hand or electric. A heavy duty stapler will deal with more pages.
- **Crimper** – the pages are crimped together by machine at the top corner, thus holding them together.

- **Hole punched** and a **treasury tag** used to hold the pages together. Alternatively, pages can be put in a ring binder.
- **Comb binder** – pages are hole punched lengthways and a plastic comb fastens pages at the spine.

- **Thermal binder** – heat fastens an adhesive spine to the pages to make a booklet.

- **Plastic side binding** – cheap and simple – a plastic strip is slid down the length of the pages to hold them together.

- Card may be used for the first and last pages to make a sturdy booklet. The outer pages can be **laminated** – a plastic covering is applied by a heat process.
- Special covers are available with cut out fronts. The title page shows through the cut out.

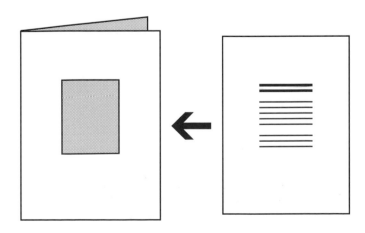

Returning finished work/deadlines

Photocopying my be requested from colleagues with specific instructions e.g.

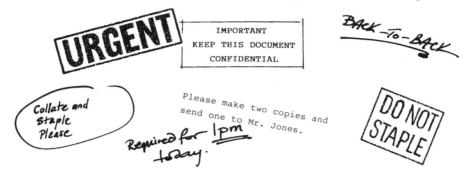

If you are unsure of any instruction, check first, before making hundreds of unwanted copies!

> **Always**
>
> ✓ Check through all instruction requests for photocopying. Those marked urgent etc. must be done first. Try to keep to deadlines – it could be important!
> ✓ Notify the person requesting, in a polite manner, if the request cannot be carried out – perhaps the photocopier is out of order. Do not just leave it.
> ✓ Complete any essential photocopying records (if your copier does not record these automatically).
> ✓ Finally, do check that the quality of copies is acceptable and collated documents are in the correct order – speed is no excuse for sloppy work!

'A few may have some pages missing, Mrs Pearson, but haven't I been quick!'

Confidentiality

If you are given documents to copy and are told that they are confidential, this means you are in a position of trust.

Do not

- make a point of immediately reading through them
- discuss them with anyone else
- leave them lying around near the photocopier for others to see
- discard wasted copies into the paper bin.

If you cannot hand the original and photocopies back to the person who requested the copying immediately, put them in a sealed envelope, addressed to that person and marked 'confidential'.

Copyright law

Just as you will be breaking the law if you copy a idea or music tape, similarly you must not copy a published document or pages from a book, unless copyright has been waived.

You and your organisation can be prosecuted under the **Copyright, Designs and Patents Act 1988** if you do!

Schools and colleges may have permission to copy certain pages from some books – make sure you check first!

Ordering and storage of materials

You will be most unpopular if you have to notify your colleagues that they cannot use the copier because the photocopy paper has run out!

Remember

- Order new paper stocks well before current stocks are used.
- Anticipate how much paper is generally used each month and order accordingly.
- Ask colleagues to let you know well in advance of any excessively large numbers of copies being required, then you can order extra supplies.
- Keep smaller stocks of coloured paper, card, labels and OHP transparencies.
- Anticipate what stocks you should keep of
  - absorbent cleaning paper rolls
  - toner
  - empty toner cartridges for used powder.
  - glass cleaning polish
  - book binding consumables

Paper should be stored in locations which are

- dry
- at room temperature
- not exposed to direct sunlight
- clean.

Keep paper in the wrapper and lying flat. Unwrapped paper may become damp and curl, resulting in paper misfeeds.

Complete the sentences below, using each of the following words *once* only.

plain	waste	rental
metal	toner	copyright
trained	fastened	reprography
scanner		

1 To photocopy pages from a book is against the _____ law.

2 Plates for offset litho duplicating can be made of paper or _____.

3 Photocopiers use _____ paper.

4 The process of reproducing documents is known as _____.

5 When copies are faint, the photocopier needs more _____.

6 An offset litho duplicator needs a _____ operator.

7 The majority of photocopiers are acquired on _____.

8 Masters for an ink duplicator can be prepared using a _____.

9 Care should be taken to keep _____ to a minimum.

10 Multi-page documents can be _____ using a variety of methods.

Wordsearch

Look at the grid below and find the following words.

DUPLICATING

COLLATE

OFFSET LITHO

THERMAL

DEADLINES

URGENT

COPYRIGHT

STAPLE

REPROGRAPHY

STENCIL

D	B	H	C	U	R	H	W	L	I	T	C
Z	O	F	F	S	E	T	L	I	T	H	O
U	R	G	E	N	T	P	T	N	S	E	P
B	S	T	A	P	L	E	L	E	P	R	Y
C	X	Y	K	S	T	J	N	F	G	M	R
J	M	V	T	A	D	I	P	C	N	A	I
X	K	T	L	K	L	F	R	K	I	L	G
F	D	L	D	D	C	L	O	G	D	L	H
B	O	M	A	F	L	Y	F	F	U	I	T
C	R	E	P	R	O	G	R	A	P	H	Y
K	D	U	P	L	I	C	A	T	I	N	G

8 Handle mail

8.1 Receive, sort and distribute mail

This section covers

▶ receiving mail
▶ opening the mail
▶ mail-opening equipment

▶ recording remittances
▶ circulating mail (using lists)
▶ suspicious letters and packages.

The Post Office is now split into three separate businesses

● Royal Mail
● Royal Mail Parcelforce
● Post Office Counters Ltd.

Receiving mail

The procedure for opening the mail will depend on the size of the organisation.

In a large company, there could be a special mailroom, staffed by people whose main job is to receive incoming and despatch outgoing mail.

Many of the larger companies have a **post box number** and a messenger will collect the sacks of mail early each morning from the local sorting office instead of waiting for it to be delivered.

Other types of mail which will be dealt with will include

● internal mail – passed between departments
● parcel deliveries
● registered and recorded deliveries
● hand deliveries
● deliveries by private courier
● messages sent by fax.

In a small office, the manager or secretary will open all mail and probably deal with most of it personally.

Opening the mail

It is important that mail is opened, sorted and distributed quickly.

● Take out letters marked *private*, *personal* or *confidential*. Do *not* open these letters!
● Open letters marked *urgent* first, then first class letters, followed by second class mail.
  Printed circulars and magazines should be opened last of all.
● Deal with each letter and enclosures *before* opening the next one, to prevent confusion.
● Date stamp all letters and documents. (Make sure you have changed the date on the stamp!)

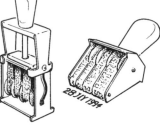

- Check that all enclosures are included and either clip or staple them to the accompanying letter or document.
  Make a note on the document if any are missing.
- Envelopes containing remittances (payments) – cash, cheques or postal orders – should be recorded in the **remittances book** and handed to a senior person for safety.
- Sort all mail into baskets or pigeon holes for the various departments and individuals, ready for delivering or collection.

- Re-check all envelopes to make sure they are empty. It is a good idea to open all envelopes flat. Some firms keep these envelopes for several days in case of queries.

- Letters delivered by hand should be opened and distributed as soon as they arrive.
- Damaged parcels should not be accepted or, alternatively, should be signed for as 'damaged on delivery'.

Mail-opening equipment

Envelopes need to be opened quickly and neatly. Avoid tearing the contents.

- A **paper knife** can be used to slit open the top edge of the envelope. Take care not to tear the enclosures.
- An **electric letter opener** slices off a narrow strip from the top of each envelope. To avoid damaging the contents, envelopes should first be tapped on the desk to allow the contents to drop to the bottom.

An electric letter opener

Recording remittances

Most organisations have some way of recording remittances received through the post.

Many firms enter details of cash, cheques and postal orders into a **remittances book**. The name of the person or firm sending the remittance is also recorded. The cashier countersigns the page when the remittances are handed over.

REMITTANCES BOOK	DATE 14 September 199-			
Name of sender	Method of payment	Amount £	p	Signature
Andrew King	Cheque	43	50	J Ryan
Cunliffe & Partners	Cheque	840	00	J Ryan
S Hunter	Cash	20	00	J Ryan
Banks & Sons Ltd	Cheque	270	90	J Ryan
P TAYLOR	CHQ	95	00	R Entwistle
M DAVIS	PO	5	00	R Entwistle
Cashier's signature K Mason				

Your tutor will give you a page from a remittances book (page 194). The remittances listed below have been received in today's post. Enter these details on the page. Your tutor will countersign the page as cashier.

- Cheque for £426.50 from Calvert Bros – account number 67245
- Cash for £80 by registered post from K Higson – account number 23694
- £73.96 by cheque from Paul Banks – account number 32463
- Anwar Hussain sent a cheque for £32.80 – account number 34895
- Cheque for £895 from P O'Brien – account number 12423
- Registered letter containing £65 cash from S Anderson – account number 23574
- Postal order for £5 from T Dickinson – account number 43286

Circulating mail

Sometimes a letter received in the mail has to be seen urgently by more than one person.

A **distribution list** can be written neatly on the letter. The letter is then photocopied – one copy for each of the names on the distribution list. Tick the person's name to whom the copy is being sent.

Magazines and bulky reports which cannot be copied usually have a **routing** or **circulation** list attached.

CIRCULATION LIST

Name	Date rec'd	Date passed on
Simon Tate	12/6/9-	12/6/9-
M Ahmed	12/6/9-	14/6/9-
Sarah Carter	14/6/9-	
Paul O'Brien		
Lisa Carter		

Please return to Admin Manager after circulation

Suspicious letters and packages

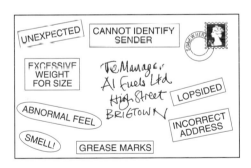

UNEXPECTED CANNOT IDENTIFY SENDER

EXCESSIVE WEIGHT FOR SIZE

ABNORMAL FEEL

SMELL! GREASE MARKS

LOPSIDED INCORRECT ADDRESS

The Manager, Al Fuels Ltd, High Street, BRIGTOWN

BE ALERT ... check all

mail arriving at your desk or home

Update on dealing with suspicious mail

! Some organisations are potential targets for this type of mail. Staff working in such places are specifically instructed to take extra care and to be diligent at all times.
! The Royal Mail letter and parcels offices have special screening equipment which scans mail.
! Information leaflets and advice on how to deal with suspicious mail can be obtained free from your local Crime Prevention Officer.
! If you receive a letter or package which causes concern, inform your supervisor or a senior person *immediately*.

Do not attempt to open the package!

Complete the sentences below, using each of the following words once only.

routeing   damage
confidential   remittances
urgent   internal
sorted   suspicious
envelopes   knife

1 As well as dealing with letters which are delivered through the post, the mailroom staff also sort _____ mail.

2 Letters marked _____ should on no account be opened.

3 A paper _____ can be used to open envelopes.

4 It is wise to keep _____ for several days in case there is a need to refer to them.

5 Letters marked _____ should be opened immediately.

6 When accepting delivery of parcels, they should be checked for _____.

7 When all the mail has been opened, it should be _____ quickly into baskets or pigeon holes.

8 A circulation list is sometimes referred to as a _____ list.

9 It is wise to record all cash, cheques and postal orders in a _____ book.

10 Royal Mail letters and parcels offices have special equipment to screen for _____ mail.

Wordsearch

Look at the grid and find the following words.

CONFIDENTIAL

FAX

REMITTANCES

PIGEON

CIRCULATE

ROUTEING

COURIER

MESSENGER

PRIVATE

BASKET

S	M	D	R	H	N	C	J	P	L	Q	C
A	E	F	B	D	Q	O	P	V	S	O	S
D	S	T	H	P	I	G	E	O	N	S	E
D	S	B	C	V	X	Q	U	F	B	L	C
E	E	R	O	U	T	E	I	N	G	B	N
X	N	S	Q	W	X	D	W	Q	B	V	A
L	G	N	C	M	E	Y	P	Q	S	J	T
B	E	M	J	N	C	B	A	S	K	E	T
B	R	J	T	N	K	L	U	I	O	R	I
Q	C	I	R	C	U	L	A	T	E	B	M
F	A	X	B	N	P	R	I	V	A	T	E
L	B	Q	R	T	C	O	U	R	I	E	R

8.2 Dispatch mail

This section covers

▶ putting letters and enclosures into envelopes
▶ mailroom procedure
▶ addressing envelopes
▶ wrapping parcels
▶ Royal Mail services
▶ postage book
▶ mailroom equipment.

As soon as the incoming mail has been distributed, mailroom staff should switch their attention to the outgoing mail.

To avoid a last minute rush of mail having to be dealt with, outgoing mail should be collected at regular intervals throughout the day.

Internal mail within the organisation can be collected and distributed at the same time.

Many firms impose a final deadline for collection of outgoing mail. Nothing is more annoying than being asked to send a letter by special mail at 5pm.

Putting letters and enclosures into envelopes

If it is the job of the mailroom staff to put letters into envelopes, care should be taken to

● check that all enclosures are attached to the letter
● check that the letter is signed
● insert the letter into the *correct* envelope, making as few folds as possible.

Window envelopes are often used nowadays and care should be taken to ensure that the name and address are fully visible. Using window envelopes avoids the error of putting a letter into the wrong envelope, and saves time.

Mailroom procedure

● Check that all envelopes are sealed. *Never* lick envelopes! Use a roller moistener to seal flaps.
● Separate all items of special mail.
● Sort mail into first and second class, keeping similar-sized envelopes together.
● Weigh any mail which feels heavier than 60g and any letters which are going abroad.
● Calculate the postage for these letters and mark the amount in pencil in one corner of the envelope.
● Complete any forms for special items of mail, then weigh and calculate the postage.
● Frank the mail or attach the correct postage stamps.
● Put franked mail in special large envelopes marked 'franked mail' ready for taking to the Post Office.

Note: Postage stamps are *always* fixed to the top right-hand corner of an envelope.

Addressing envelopes

The most popular size of envelope used in business is DL size which takes A4 paper folded equally into three.

DL envelopes are available in three styles.

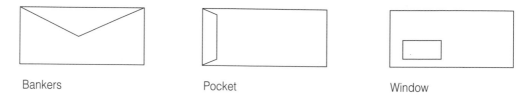

Bankers   Pocket   Window

Many firms have their name and address printed either in the left-hand corner of the envelope or on the opening flap.

An undelivered letter can quickly be returned to the sender.

Adhesive address labels are often used to stick on envelopes as these can be produced quickly by computer.

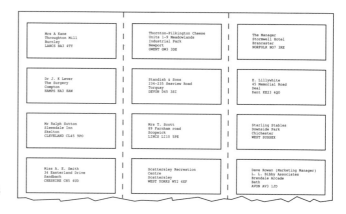

Computer address labels

Companies which use window envelopes have their letter head paper marked with two dots (or some other mark). The name and address is typed between the two marks.

When the letter is folded and inserted in the envelope, the addressee details show clearly through the window.

Ask your tutor for a window envelope and a sheet of marked letter head paper.

Type your own name and address on the letter where indicated

Practise folding the letter and inserting it in the envelope so that your name and address is clearly visible through the window.

Rules to follow

- Make sure that the envelope is sufficiently large to take the letter *and* any enclosures.
- It is preferable to type envelopes. If handwritten, they should be neat and clear.
- On DL and smaller envelopes, use single line spacing, blocked style. Double line spacing would be clearer on larger envelopes.
- The name and address should be started halfway down and about one-third in from the left edge.
- Always put the postal town in capitals. It is preferable to put the postcode on a separate line with no punctuation. (Punctuation can slow down the Royal Mail mechanised letter sorting process.)

```
Mrs Ann Wood
31 Kay Street
CHORLEY
BB7 2KL
```

- Envelopes for overseas mail should have the town (or city) and the country in capitals.
- Special mailing and addressee instructions are positioned as shown in the illustrations below.

```
Mr John Davis

27 Fountain

Avenue

CHORLEY

DB7 4FW
```

RECORDED DELIVERY

```
Mr Paul Sager
4 Ceder Avenue
MANCHESTER
M5 6YR
```

The same applies for registered post, special delivery and par avion (by airmail)

```
PERSONAL
Mr T King
464 Green Park
BIRMINGHAM
BM2 5KL
```

The same applies for personal, confidential and urgent

```
FOR THE ATTENTION OF MR T DAY
Messrs Crabtree & Page
16 High Street
EDINBURGH
EH1 4PL
```

```
Express Orders Ltd
FREEPOST
Canterbury House
EDINBURGH
EH2 5WS
```

Ask your tutor for a selection of different-sized envelopes. Folded A4 paper could be used as a substitute.

Prepare envelopes, preferably typed, for the following addresses. Start a new line where two spaces have been left between items.

For special mailing and addressee instructions check the layout with the illustrations on page 127.

1 Mrs Pauline Butterworth   Alston & Company   44 Butler Street   NORWICH
Norfolk   NR2 6QR

2 Dr David Hanson   Brierfield Health Centre   Stanley Street   EDINBURGH
EH16 5BU

3 Studio 72   Ramsgreave House   York Road   GRANTHAM   Lincs   NG3 6RZ

4 Mr B Atherton   15 Junction Road   PRESTON   Lancs   PR3 9TX
(Mark the envelope SPECIAL DELIVERY)

5 Leisure Wear Ltd   27 Deansgate   MANCHESTER   M4 3ES
(Mark the envelope FOR THE ATTENTION OF MR JACK CLAYTON)

6 Mr Stuart Kendal   Lincoln Chambers   47 Main Street   LONDON   SW6 3PR
(Mark the envelope CONFIDENTIAL)

7 The Manager   Associated Systems Ltd   546 Planet Road   FARNBOROUGH
Hants   GU14 7NU
(Mark the envelope URGENT)

Wrapping parcels

The mailroom should keep a selection of the following materials for wrapping parcels:

brown paper	polystyrene chips
strong cardboard boxes	a supply of old newspapers
assorted size jiffy (padded) bags	adhesive tape (various widths)
bubble wrap	string
corrugated paper	scissors

Rules to follow

- Use stout card to protect photographs, certificates etc.
- Jiffy bags are quick and handy for sending unbreakable items such as books.
- Wrap fragile articles first with one of the wrapping materials listed above, before placing them in a cardboard box. Make sure the articles can withstand bumps and rough handling. Label **Fragile – with care!**
- Secure the box generously with adhesive tape or string.
- Label the parcel clearly, following the layout rules for addressing letters on page 127.
- Put the sender's name and address on the outside of the parcel in case it cannot be delivered for some reason.

For more information about sending articles by post, obtain the booklet *Wrapping up Well* from the Royal Mail.

Royal Mail services

There are several different ways of sending letters, packets and parcels through the post. The main services are listed below.

Letter Post

- *First class post* – delivered the day after collection
- *Second class post* – delivered by the third working day after collection
- *Certificate of posting* – gives proof of posting only

Priority services

For speed

- *Special delivery* – next day delivery by 12.30pm to most UK destinations
- *Datapost* – next day delivery

For valuable items

- *Registered* – next day delivery by 12.30 pm to most UK destinations; compensation up to a maximum of £500; signature obtained on delivery
- *Registered plus* – given extra security procedures; next day delivery by 5.30 pm to most UK destinations; compensation up to a maximum of £2200 ; signature obtained on delivery

For important items

- *Recorded delivery* – use to send **important** documents (not valuables); signature obtained on delivery

For proof of delivery

- *Advice of delivery* – a proof of delivery card is returned to the sender; can be used with special delivery, registered or recorded delivery mail

Reply services

- *Business reply service* – customers can reply without paying for postage; envelopes or postcards are printed with a special design showing the licence number
- *Freepost* – again saves customers paying for postage 'Freepost' is included in the address

International

- *Registered* – use for **valuable** items: 2-tier compensation. up to £500 or £1000; signature obtained on delivery
- *Recorded delivery* – use for **important** items: compensation up to £24 only; signature obtained on delivery
- *Aerogrammes/pictorial aerogrammes* – all-in-one stationery, incorporating the cost of the stamp
- *Airmail* – use to send mail abroad quickly; lightweight mail to EU countries will go at a special rate; (outside Europe, use an Airmail label or write 'Par avion – By airmail' on the envelope)
- *Swiftair Express* – use for sending urgent mail abroad quickly (Pre-paid envelopes called SWIFTPACKS are now available to send anywhere in the world.)

- *Datapost* – a very fast service for sending mail abroad; next day delivery to Europe, 48 hours to many other countries
- *Airstream* – for companies which send large quantities of mail abroad

Parcels (UK)

- *Parcelforce Datapost 10* – guaranteed delivery by 10 am next working day
- *Parcelforce Datapost 12* – guaranteed delivery by noon next working day
- *Parcelforce 24* – guaranteed delivery by close of business next working day
- *Parcelforce 48* – guaranteed delivery within 2 working days
- *Parcelforce standard* – delivery normally within 3 working days
- *Compensation fee parcel* – use to send **valuable** parcels; compensation up to £20, £150 or £500 depending upon the fee paid

Parcels International

- *International Datapost* – guaranteed express delivery worldwide; next day to most of Europe and within 48 hours to many other countries
- *International Standard* – worldwide delivery to over 214 countries; 5 working days to Europe, 7 working days to the rest of the world
- *International Economy* – worldwide delivery to over 214 countries; 10 working days to Europe, 20 working days to the rest of the world

Private delivery services

There are other **private carriers** who will deliver packages and parcels.

British Rail Red Star offer an ordinary station-to-station next day parcel delivery service, or a more expensive same day delivery for urgent parcels.

Look under PARCEL DELIVERY in your local *Yellow Pages*.

You will be referred (cross-referenced) to

- Courier services
- Delivery and collection services
- Post Offices
- Railway stations and offices

Make a list of *ten* private carriers, together with their addresses and telephone numbers.

As a group, obtain the following booklets from the Royal Mail.

- *UK Letter Rates*
- *Royal Mail International – The easy way to mail abroad*
- *Parcelforce – A concise guide to services and prices for UK and international services.*

Use these booklets to find more detailed information on the Royal Mail services listed above.

Up-to-date charges are given for the mailing services.

Postage book

Although many companies now have franking machines for stamping the outgoing mail, smaller offices still use postage stamps. A record therefore should be kept of all outgoing mail, together with the cost of postage.

Because of the volume of first and second class letters, this type of mail must be batched and recorded in the **postage book** as '56 1st class letters' or '23 2nd class letters'.

Details of special mail, however, is recorded in the book together with the value of stamps used. Additional fees for special mail are usually taken from petty cash. Receipts obtained from the Post Office are generally clipped to the postage book or given to the petty cashier.

An example of the postage book is shown below.

Date	Stamps bought	Addressee	Stamps used	Special mail	Fees from petty cash
	£ p				£ p
12 Aug	55.00	Balance b/f			
		56 1st class letters	13.44		
		23 2nd class letters	4.14		
		J Quinn Dover	49		
		L Peters York	24	Rec dely	30
		K Mitchell Detroit USA	57	Airmail	
		R Westwell Cardiff	24	Spec dely	1.95
		S Saunders Bath	2.28	parcel	
			21.40		
		Balance c/f	33.60		
	55.00		55.00		

The book is balanced either daily or weekly.

Mailroom equipment

Postage scales

Modern postage scales are electronic. They are fitted with a special chip and, when certain keys are pressed, they will work out the weight and rate of postage for most types of mail.

electronic postage scale

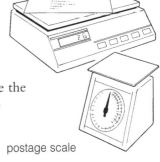
postage scale

- When postage rates change, the chip has to be replaced by the manufacturer.
- Ordinary postage scales can be used but they will just give the weight of the letter or packet. You will have to check the amount of postage payable by referring to an up-to-date Royal Mail postal charges booklet.

Franking machines

Instead of affixing postage stamps to envelopes, the machine prints the amount of postage payable on to the envelope.

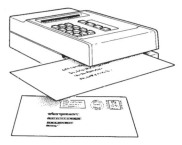

franking machine

● For parcels, a stick-on label is printed with the correct postage.
● For security, the machine should be locked when not in use.
● An advertising slogan of the company can be incorporated into the franked impression.
● Franking machines are hired or purchased from manufacturers.
● A licence for a machine must be obtained from the Post Office.
● Postage units are purchased from the Post Office and set into the machine.
● A meter displays the number of units remaining in the machine. This number decreases each time the machine is used.
● When the machine is empty, more units are purchased in advance from the Post Office.
● Units can be set into later models electronically by telephoning the manufacturer for a special code to key in to the machine.
● A franking control card is completed daily to record usage. The card must be sent to the Post Office each week.
● The date on the machine must be changed daily and more ink added when the franked impression fades.
● The amount of postage required is selected by changing dials.
● Envelopes or labels stamped in error can be saved and returned to the Post Office for credit.
● Franked mail must be put in special large envelopes marked 'Franked mail' and handed over the counter at the Post Office. It should *not* be put in an ordinary post box.

franked mail

Note: Even though a company may frank all of its outgoing mail, a small supply of postage stamps should be kept for emergency use.

Inserting, folding, sealing machines

● These machines automatically fold and insert letters and enclosures into envelopes, before sealing them. Have you ever wondered how gas, electricity and telephone bills are folded and inserted so neatly into envelopes?

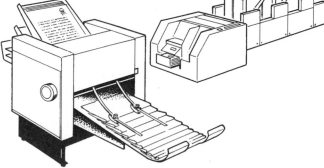

Complete the sentences below, using each of the following words *once* only.

Parcelforce   scales   cardboard
enclosures   registered   postage
jiffy   window   internal
envelope

1 Whilst collecting the outgoing mail for dispatch, the _____ mail can also be collected, ready for sorting and delivering to other departments.

2 When putting letters into envelopes for dispatching by mail, care should be taken to attach all _____.

3 By using _____ envelopes, the error of putting letters into the wrong envelope is avoided.

4 The term DL refers to a size of _____.

5 The Royal Mail business now dealing with parcels is called ____ .

6 To send valuable items by mail, _____ post should be used.

7 To send unbreakable items through the post, special padded packets called _____ bags can be bought from the Post Office and stationers.

8 The _____ book is used to keep a record of outgoing mail and the number of stamps used.

9 The latest postage _____ contain a chip which can calculate the amount of postage payable.

10 Fragile articles should first be wrapped securely, then packed into a stout _____ box before mailing.

Wordsearch

Look at the grid below and find the following words.

REGISTERED

MAILROOM

FREEPOST

RECORDED

DATAPOST

FRANKING

DEADLINE

SWIFTAIR

STAMP

AIRMAIL

M	A	I	L	R	O	O	M	L	D	P
D	R	E	H	J	F	D	S	I	E	M
G	V	E	N	H	G	F	R	A	A	A
N	W	Q	G	H	O	J	G	M	D	T
I	F	S	H	I	J	T	A	R	L	S
K	G	J	P	F	S	H	K	I	I	O
N	E	R	H	J	D	T	W	A	N	P
A	D	U	P	L	N	M	E	F	E	A
R	S	W	I	F	T	A	I	R	S	T
F	R	E	E	P	O	S	T	T	E	A
S	D	G	R	E	C	O	R	D	E	D

Monitor and issue stock items

9.1 Monitor and request stock

This section covers

▶ stock consumables
▶ storage of stationery items
▶ safety in the stock room
▶ issuing stock/stationery requisitions.

Stock consumables

When you have become competent at carrying out routine clerical tasks, you may find that your supervisor asks you to undertake additional duties – sometimes making you responsible for certain jobs.

This generally means that your work to date has been satisfactory and your supervisor feels that you are capable of taking on extra responsibility – that of making sure the office does not run out of stationery items.

If a factory runs out of raw materials, production will automatically stop. It is equally important that offices do not run out of essential items such as paper, envelopes, typewriter ribbons etc. These items are known as **consumables** because they need replacing on a regular basis.

'I've typed all those letters like you asked, Mrs Pearson. Can't send them out until next week 'cos we've run out of envelopes!'

What are consumables?

Can you supply the missing letters to identify the consumable items listed below?

1 A4 b_ _d p_p_r

2 A4 b_n_ p_ _ _r

3 l_t_ _r he_d p_ _ _r

4 _arb_n p_ _ _r

5 c_rd

6 l_b_ls

7 _n_ _l_p_s

8 m_ss_g_ p_ds

9 d_c_m_ _t _ _l_ _rs

10 p_nc_ls

11 ba_l _oin_ p_ns

12 c_rr_ _ti_n fl_ _d

13 adh_ _ _ve t_ _e

14 st_p_ _rs and s_ _pl_ _

15 _c_ss_rs

16 h_ _ _ p_nch_ _

17 r_bb_ _ st_m_ _

18 b_lld_g c_ _p_

19 p_ _ _ _ cl_ps

20 _l_st_c _ands

Can you think of any additional items to add to the above list?

Look at the following illustrations of consumable items. Can you identify them?

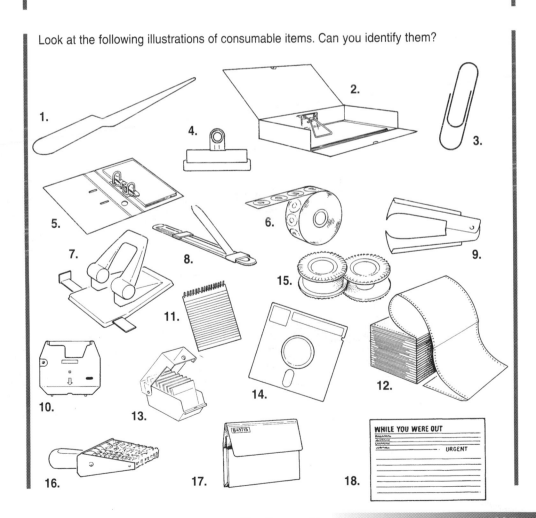

Storage of stationery items

Depending upon the size of your workplace, stationery is kept in either a stock room or a stationery cupboard.

> Why do you think it is important that both the stock room and stationery cupboard are kept locked at all times?

Shelves in stock rooms and stationery cupboards must be clearly labelled to show where each item can quickly be found. This will also help to identify where new stock should be placed.

Stock room

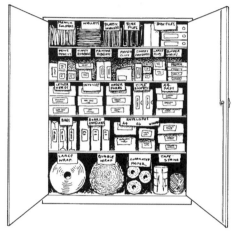

Stationery store cupboard

All boxes and packets on shelves should be clearly marked with bold lettering to show the contents of each.

Safety in the stock room

Remember

! *Always* use safety steps or a safety stool when placing or reaching items from top shelves.

 ! No smoking in the stock room.

! Keep the stock room tidy. Throw away all empty boxes.

! Make sure that **flammable** (will easily burn) liquids are clearly labelled and stored away from heat.

! Thinners and ammonia which are sometimes used in copying machines should be kept in a well-ventilated area as they can give off dangerous fumes.

Explain to your tutor why

1 Large, bulky items should be stored either on the floor or on the bottom shelves.

2 Items requested regularly should be stored within easy reach, not on top shelves or behind other items.

3 Small items, such as erasers, correction fluid and drawing pins should be placed at the front, never behind larger items.

4 Pens and pencils should be stood upright in a box – not laid flat on shelves.

5 New stock should be placed either underneath or behind old stock.

6 Paper should always be kept in a dry, well-ventilated room, which has adequate lighting.

Issuing stock/stationery requisitions

You will almost certainly have other duties to carry out in addition to issuing stationery to staff. It is therefore more convenient to keep a regular day and time when your colleagues know they will be able to obtain supplies of stationery from the stockroom or cupboard.

This distribution can be organised in several ways:

● Each week staff can write their stationery requirements for the coming week in a stationery book which is circulated around the various offices and then returned to you.

● Staff can write a note to you listing the items they will need for the coming week. This type of note is called a **stationery requisition**. Supplies of these requisitions are kept by staff who will complete one when stationery is required. Each requisition is printed with a consecutive number.

Look below. Simon Ward has requested four calculator batteries.

Simon has had to ask his departmental manager, Georgia Kingston, to approve his requisition.

Can you think of a reason why her approval is needed?

STATIONERY REQUISITION	
FROM *Simon Ward* DATE *23/10/199-*	
DEPT *Accounts* REQ NO 621	
Please supply:	
Quantity	Item
4	*Calculator batteries*
Signed: *Simon Ward*	
Approved by: *Georgia Kingston*	

Your tutor will give you *four* blank stationery requisitions (page 195).

Complete a requisition from each of the following people who are requesting stationery items for the coming week.

Do not sign the requisitions but remember to date each one for 17 November.

Requisition No 731

from   Mark Greenwood of the Technical Dept

for   4 packets of A4 bond paper
                                                          1 box staples

Requisition No 732

from   Sarah Longworth of the Secretarial Dept

for   5 packets of A4 bond paper
                                                          6 bottles of correction fluid
                                                          4 reams of A4 letter head paper

Requisition No 733

from   Hanif Sidat of the Sales Dept

for   8 packets of A4 bond paper

Requisition No 734

from   Jennifer Thomas of the Admin Dept

for   1 ream of A4 letter head paper
                                                          6 bottles of correction fluid
                                                          2 boxes of staples

When you have received the requisitions you can assemble the stationery orders, which staff can either collect at a specified time or you can deliver to them.

A notice displayed on the door of the stock room or stationery cupboard will remind staff of the arrangements for the issue of stationery.

Design a notice for display advising the staff that stationery will be issued only on Tuesdays and Fridays between 0930 and 1030.

Requisitions must be received by you before 1600 the day before.

(Why not use a letter stencil or Letraset to design your notice? Have you any calligraphy skills? Can you design and print out a notice using your computer? It could look more professional than using free-hand skills!)

Fill in the gaps in the following sentences. Choose only *one* of the two words shown at the end of each sentence.

1 A _____ is completed by someone requesting an item of stock. (**record, requisition**)

2 Stock items which can easily burn are referred to as _____. (**ventilated, flammable**)

3 To help find stock items quickly in the stationery cupboard, all boxes should be _____. (**labelled, replaced**)

4 Use safety _____ when reaching stock items from high shelves. (**ladders, boxes**)

5 Staff should not be allowed to _____ in the stock room. (**talk, smoke**)

6 _____ stock should always be placed either underneath or behind existing stock. (**old, new**)

7 You must store large, bulky items on the _____ shelves. (**bottom, top**)

8 _____ is a liquid sometimes used in copying machines. (**ammonia, water**)

9 A _____ is used to make holes in paper before filing. (**stapler, punch**)

10 Good quality paper is called _ _ paper. (**bank, bond**)

Wordsearch

Look at the grid below and find the following words.

CONSUMABLES

PUNCH

SCISSORS

ENVELOPES

SAFETY

REQUISITIONS

RECORDS

FLAMMABLE

RIBBONS

STATIONERY

R	E	Q	U	I	S	I	T	I	O	N	S
E	C	G	W	N	X	Z	J	O	P	E	A
C	F	L	S	C	N	W	Q	R	L	Q	M
O	I	H	N	A	R	I	B	B	O	N	S
R	L	C	B	M	X	S	A	F	E	T	Y
D	K	N	F	L	A	M	M	A	B	L	E
S	C	U	Q	P	U	K	H	F	T	Y	A
X	B	P	K	S	C	I	S	S	O	R	S
H	V	E	N	V	E	L	O	P	E	S	B
S	Q	O	B	V	H	K	G	R	T	Y	E
O	C	S	T	A	T	I	O	N	E	R	Y
V	T	R	U	T	Q	W	H	N	B	C	P

9.2 Issue stock items on request

This section covers

▶ stock records
▶ reordering new stock (including emergency orders)
▶ receipt of new stock (including legislation)
▶ recording new stock
▶ stock checking (reconciliation)
▶ annual stock-taking
▶ computerised stock records.

Stock records

It is important that you know exactly how much stationery there is in stock. To avoid having to count each individual item, a record card is usually kept for each stock item.

The record cards are generally kept in a card index box and filed in **alphabetical** order of stock item.

Each time an item of stationery is issued, this should be recorded on the appropriate record card.

See below how the requisition for four calculator batteries from Simon Ward as shown on page 137 is recorded on the record card.

STATIONERY RECORD CARD

ITEM: ......*CALCULATOR BATTERIES*........... MAX: ..*100*....

SUPPLIER: *SUMMIT LIGHTING COMPANY* MIN: ..*20*.....

Date	Quantity received	Quantity issued	Dept	Req No	Balance in stock
1 Oct					24
23 Oct		4	Accounts	621	20

Look at the 'balance in stock' figure shown on the above record card. There are only 20 batteries left in stock, which is the minimum balance shown at the top of the card.

This serves as a reminder for you to order more batteries to prevent running out of stock. Your regular supplier of batteries is also shown at the top of the card.

Inform your tutor

1 how many calculator batteries should be ordered to restore the balance in stock to the maximum number.

2 the name of the supplier of these batteries.

Ordering too many batteries should be avoided (even if they can be purchased much more cheaply) because they

● can deteriorate in quality
● can become out of date
● tie up the firm's capital (money)
● take up valuable storage space.

'I've ordered 10 000 boxes of batteries, Mrs Pearson, 'cos they were less than half the usual price!'

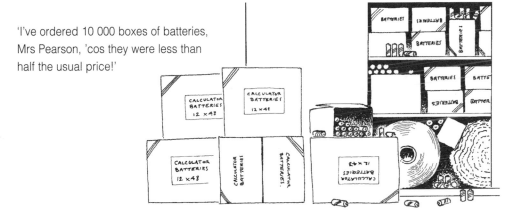

Your tutor will give you *four* stationery record cards on which have been recorded previously issued items (page 196). Each card shows the up-to-date balance in stock. Using the four requisitions which you completed earlier from the details given on page 138, you should

1 Enter each item of stationery on to the respective record card. Calculate the up-to-date balance in stock after each entry.

2 After all four stationery requisitions have been recorded on the record cards and balances recalculated, inform your tutor which stationery items have reached their minimum balance and therefore need re-ordering.

Have you re-calculated the balances on the stationery cards correctly?

Re-ordering new stock

Stationery can be re-ordered in either of two ways

● by sending a note of your requirements to your Purchasing Department. (This type of note is called a **purchase requisition**.) *or*
● by sending an **order form** to your usual supplier direct.

Very occasionally, stationery may need to be re-ordered in an emergency. This could occur when several departments have requested the same stock item during the same week. In this instance, telephoning the supplier would be the quickest way of receiving supplies.

Receipt of new stock

When new stock is received, this should be carefully checked for discrepancies which could mean

- missing items
- damaged items
- additional items sent in error
- incorrect items.

It is important to check that the items actually delivered match those listed on the **goods delivery note**.

If an error is discovered, the supplier should be contacted immediately so that the error can be pointed out.

Note: The **Sale of Goods Act 1979** protects buyers of goods. The legislation states that goods for sale must be

- as described
- of merchantable quality
- fit for the purpose for which they are intended.

The **Trade Descriptions Act 1968** states that it is an offence to give a false description.

Recording new stock

Let us assume that we re-ordered a supply of calculator batteries when the number in stock had fallen to the minimum balance on the stationery record card, shown on page 140. To restore the balance to the maximum number, we should have ordered 80 batteries. See how this delivery would be recorded on the record card shown below

STATIONERY RECORD CARD

ITEM: ...CALCULATOR..BATTERIES........... MAX:..100....

SUPPLIER: SUMMIT..LIGHTING..COMPANY. MIN:..20.....

Date	Quantity received	Quantity issued	Dept	Req No	Balance in stock
1 Oct					24
23 Oct		4	Accounts	621	20
30 Oct	80				100

Using the stationery record cards previously completed by you, you should now

1 Record the receipt of the stock items listed below on the respective record card.

Remember, all stock received is recorded in the 'quantity received' column and not the 'quantity issued' column. The new stock was received on 29 November.

Stock received
456 packets of A4 bond paper
40 boxes of staples
251 reams of A4 letter head paper

2 Calculate the up-to-date balances on each stationery record card.

Stock checking (reconciliation)

Even though an up-to-date balance of each stock item can be found on the respective stationery record card, it is important that the *actual* stock is checked at regular intervals. This check is often called an **inventory reconciliation**. Any stock which has deteriorated, been damaged or become out of date can be found during a stock check.

This stock check will also reveal whether the balances on the record cards are correct and, more important, whether any stock has been pilfered (stolen).

If any shortages (these are often called **discrepancies**) are found, the supervisor must be informed *immediately* and the matter investigated further.

Annual stock-taking

At least once a year, all stock is checked thoroughly. A list is made of all items and the value of the stock is calculated to show how much of the firm's capital is tied up in stock.

This valuation is required by the firm's **auditors** who can work out how much money is being spent each year on consumable items.

Can you suggest how the firm can find out which department has been using most stationery items?

Computerised stock records

Many firms have computerised their stock records. Upon receipt, data about all new stock is entered into the computer and the balances are automatically adjusted.

All stationery items issued to staff are also recorded. The total amount of stock held is therefore always immediately available.

Stock-control programs quickly identify which stock needs re-ordering. However, a manual stock check must still be made once a year – sometimes more regularly.

Fill in the missing letters and then write the completed words in your folder to help you remember what they mean.

1 A note given to the stationery clerk asking for supplies of stationery is called a stationery r_qu_s_t_on.

2 An item of stationery which is used in an office and needs to be replaced regularly is called a con_____.

3 Care should be taken when storing dangerous materials in the stock room. Two words which can be used to describe these dangerous materials are haz___ous and fl__m_b__.

4 Stock which is out of date is often referred to as obs___te stock.

5 Sometimes stationery needs to be ordered very quickly because stocks are very low. The stock clerk there fore has to telephone for an em__g__c_ order.

6 The stock clerk must be aware of laws passed by the Government when receiving new stock. The laws are often referred to as leg__lat__n.

7 When checking stationery, if the balance does not agree with the balance you expect, this is called a dis____anc_.

8 Your entries on the stationery record cards should always be readable and correct. Another way of describing your writing could be leg_b__ and a__ura__.

9 Stock should be checked at regular intervals to make sure that balances are correct, that stock has not deteriorated, been stolen, damaged or become out of date. This stock check is known as a stock rec__cil_____.

10 If stock records are completed in handwriting, this is known as man___ record keeping. If stock records are recorded on a computer, this is known as com_____ised record keeping.

Wordsearch

Look at the grid shown and find the following words.

OBSOLETE

BOND

PAPER

ELASTIC

WALLET

FOLDER

BULLDOG

CARBON

AMMONIA

DISCREPANCY

S	D	G	H	J	E	Q	E	W	P	Y	P
S	F	O	L	D	E	R	S	V	H	C	L
C	A	R	B	O	N	D	W	C	C	N	L
W	I	A	N	S	C	Q	R	T	I	A	L
Q	N	K	L	B	O	N	D	Q	T	P	M
Z	O	M	W	A	L	L	E	T	S	E	P
C	M	A	I	P	A	P	E	R	A	R	N
M	M	D	F	G	H	F	D	T	L	C	L
Q	A	V	C	S	T	Y	K	J	E	S	M
W	W	B	U	L	L	D	O	G	X	I	C
S	W	E	Y	P	N	G	F	S	A	D	C
D	K	T	W	R	T	P	L	V	X	S	W

10 Improving your writing skills

This chapter covers

▶ using correct grammar
▶ improving spelling
▶ punctuation
▶ extending vocabulary
▶ letters
▶ memos.

Many people today are not confident about writing letters and memos. You needn't be one of them. Pay attention to improving your basic **writing skills**.

Using correct grammar

You might wonder why it is important to use correct grammar. It might not be important when you are talking to your friends, but when you are writing letters for your company it is.

Letters must be clear and understandable. Every letter you send is an ambassador for the company you work for. To make sure each letter is right it is helpful to know some basic grammar, so you can check what you write is correct.

Nouns and verbs

A **noun** can be a person, place or thing.

e.g.   David,   girl,   Brighton,   kitchen,   book,   purse

A **verb** is a *doing* word which illustrates an action.

To find out whether a word is a verb, see if it makes sense with the word 'to' in front of it.

e.g.   to read   to ask
       to write   to employ

A sentence must contain at least a **noun** (subject) and a **verb** (action). If the action is being done to someone or something, that thing is the **object** of the sentence, and is also a noun or a pronoun.

e.g.   subject   verb
       Terry shouted.

       subject   verb   object
       The clerk posted the letter.

A sentence always starts with a capital letter and ends with a full stop.

Incomplete sentences

Make sure you write complete sentences, *not*

> With regard to your letter.
> Despite the interest shown.
> Because of the cost involved.

These are not complete sentences. Beware! Don't be someone who starts letters 'Dear Simon, With regard to your letter of 25 September.' Try, 'Dear Simon, Thank you for your letter of 25 September.' This second example has the verb 'thank'.

Singular and plural

Remember:

singular	plural
I am	We are
John is	Tom and Jill are
She was	They were
I was	We were

Collective nouns can cause problems.

> e.g.   group   government   class   team

The government *is* to be recalled.
A list of books *has* been given to the librarian.
A variety of papers *is* stored in the cabinet.

Only *one* government, so use a singular verb.
List is the subject of the second sentence. There's only one list even if there are many books on it, so use a singular verb.

Rewrite the following sentences correctly by changing the word in italics.

1   The children forgot to tell their mother where they *was* going.

2   Adults are *learnt* new skills to help them find work.

3   The hotel *are* offering special discounts to guests staying the night.

4   We haven't been *nowhere* for our holidays this year.

5   Which of the twins is the *tallest*?

6   Mary and June *is* going to be late for college.

Check your answer with the key.

If you have got a sentence wrong, check the mistake with your tutor.

Lots of people muddle 'learn' and 'teach/taught'. Remember, people *learn* things but a teacher must *teach* them. If you're not sure which to use, always check in your dictionary.

Don't use double negatives – *not* with *nothing, no-one, nowhere*, etc. The effect is to cancel the negative. If 'I've not got nothing' then maybe I have something! This is not the message I want to give.

Big, bigger, biggest; *good, better, best*. If you are comparing only two things (and twins come in twos) then you need only the first two adjectives: big and bigger, or tall and taller etc. If you have more than two things to compare then you need to use an adjective ending in – *est*.

e.g. Chris types faster.
      Who is the fairest of them all?

In the final sentence in the task on page 146, the subject is plural – Mary *and* Jane: *they are* both going to be late for college.

Improving spelling

Certain words which are used regularly in business correspondence are unfortunately often misspelt. It is worth taking the effort to learn troublesome words. (In the long run it will save you time because you won't need to look them up in a dictionary each time you write or type them.)

Look at the following group of words. Make sure you can spell each word correctly. Copy down those which you are unsure of.

Afterwards cover each group and ask your tutor to dictate them to you so that you can write them down.

Check carefully that you have spelt each one correctly.

Group 1 – adding 'ly'

late	lately	comparative	comparatively
sincere	sincerely	approximate	approximately
unfortunate	unfortunately	separate	separately
rare	rarely	accurate	accurately
complete	completely	extreme	extremely

Remember – just add 'ly' to the original word.

Group 2 – past tenses

			Exceptions
omit	omitted		benefited
refer	referred		answered
permit	permitted		lowered
occur	occurred		
transfer	transferred		
cancel	cancelled		
submit	submitted		
enrol	enrolled		
commit	committed		
incur	incurred		
initial	initialled		

Note – in this group of words, the consonant at the end of the original word has been doubled.

Group 3 – silent letters

Some words contain letters which are not sounded.

plumber	scissors
column	government
prompt	length
chaos	schedule (depending on pronunciation)
ghost	psychology
depot	environment

Group 4 – in words which are pronounced **ee** remember **i** before **e** except after **c**.

	After 'c'	*Exceptions*
believe	receive	seize
thief	receipt	
achieve	ceiling	
reprieve	deceive	
grievance	conceive	
hygiene		
wield		
cashier		

Group 5 – 'double trouble'

accommodation	assessment
committee	success
commission	woollen
address	occurrence
embarrass	

Group 6 – extra care needed with these words

maintenance	February	infinite
colleagues	competent	surprise
exercise	guarantee	liaison
catalogue	opportunity	separate
definite	recommend	business
necessary	signature	secretary
until	whether	procedure

Learn a group a week, and you'll soon master these difficult words.

Remember:

You should always have a dictionary handy – *if in doubt, check it out.*

Take extra care when using similar sounding words (**homonyms**). See how easy it is to choose the wrong spelling.

● I have been to t*their*re house many times.

● The girl *has* been late for work twice this week.

● The company will have to b*bear*re the cost of the accident.

● The new dress was far t*too* small.

● Come to a*our*re house for supper.

Complete the following sentences selecting the correctly spelt word.

1 WERE   WHERE   WEAR

   a I prefer to _____ a uniform for work.

   b The children_____ late for the party.

   c Let me know _____ the box has been hidden.

2 THERE   THEIR

   a We are hoping _____ will be a cancellation.

   b It has been said that dogs sometimes resemble _____ owners.

3 TO   TOO   TWO

   a The restaurant had prepared _____ many meals.

   b Can you find _____ more books for me to borrow?

   c They agreed _____ delay the start of the game.

4 AS   HAS

   a Joanne _____ seen a jacket which will match her new skirt.

   b You should always check calculations _____ it is easy to make a mistake.

5 FARE   FAIR

   a The _____ from Bristol to London has recently been increased.

   b It is not _____ when people refuse to wait their turn.

6 OF   OFF

   a They were given instructions to turn _____ the electricity.

   b Try to arrive at a new job with plenty _____ time to spare.

7 NO   KNOW

   a Can you let your supervisor _____ whether you are able to work on Saturday?

   b There will be _____ more postal deliveries today.

8 CHECK   CHEQUE

   a I made out a _____ to pay the electricity account.

   b It is a good idea to use a calculator to _____ figures.

Punctuation

CAPITAL LETTERS

● Every sentence must begin with a **capital letter** and end with a **full stop**. Occasionally, a **question mark** or **exclamation mark** can take the place of a full stop.

How did you enjoy the film?
Beware of the dog!

● **Proper nouns** always begin with **capital letters**.

James and Catherine went to Rome for their holidays.
We are going to Ramsey in the Isle of Man.
I have an interview with the Personnel Manager, Ian Kennedy.
Next year Easter falls in April.

● The word **I** is always written as a **capital letter**, whether used at the *beginning* or in the *middle* of a sentence.

I often wish that I had paid more attention at school.

Hyphens   -

A hyphen is used

● to connect two 'describing' words

well-mannered   three-sided   cost-effective

● to split a word at the end of a line.

We have arranged for the entertain-
ment after the presentation of prizes.

Dashes   –

A dash is used to give a pause within a sentence.

A receptionist should be courteous to all callers – they could be future customers.

Semi-colons   ;

A semi-colon can be used to separate two clauses in a sentence.

The sky was black; it would soon begin to rain.

Colons   :

A colon is used before introducing a list.

The girl had many interests: netball, swimming, roller-skating and tennis.

Apostrophe '

1 An apostrophe is used to show ownership

● **before** the 's', to indicate *one* owner

my dog's ball   Simon's coat

● **after** the 's', to indicate *more than one* owner.

girls' toilets   boys' classroom

When referring to units of time

● **before** the 's', if *singular*

one hour's drive   one year's pay

● **after** the 's', if *plural*

four days' wages   seven weeks' time

● **ordinary plural** words *do not* need an apostrophe.

hotels   letters   caravans   books

Exception: **It's** always means *it is*.

It's time to go.

Do *not* use the apostrophe for

The bird was in its cage.

2 An apostrophe shows that a letter or letters are missing from a word.

I have ... *I've*   who have ... *who've*
you will ... *you'll*   you have ... *you've*
there is ... *there's*   is not ... *isn't*
cannot ... *can't*   does not ... *doesn't*
have not ... *haven't*   you are ... *you're*
who would ... *who'd*   I would ... *I'd*
we are ... *we're*   who is ... *who's*
of the clock ... *o'clock*   *and of course, it is ... it's*

Rewrite the following sentences inserting apostrophes where appropriate.

● Isnt the house cold?
● I hope youll return Johns letter.
● Theres a problem with Jacks car.
● Well arrive at the managers office at 9 oclock.
● We cant decide if its going to be problem.

Extending vocabulary

When people say 'I can't write letters' what they really mean is 'I can never think of the correct words to use.'

They have a **limited vocabulary**!

Vocabulary can be extended by

● reading – books, newspapers or magazines
● listening to news programmes on TV or radio
● doing wordsearch puzzles and crosswords
● asking people to explain the meaning of an unfamiliar word
● checking the meaning of new words in a dictionary.

Why not keep a notebook with a separate page for each letter of the alphabet? Each week, make a point of writing down ten new words. After one year, you will know the meaning of 500 new words and – hopefully – be able to spell each one correctly! Just think – after five years …

Read through the sentences below. Notice the words in italics. Check their meaning in a dictionary and find an alternative word or words which mean the same.

1 The clerk said she would give the customer a *facsimile* copy.

2 The teacher agreed that the question was *ambiguous*.

3 The newspaper published the letter knowing it would *provoke* much response.

4 Several people were invited to *participate*.

5 The police could not find any evidence to *substantiate* the claim.

Letters

In business, letters are used to request and pass on information between firms and individuals.

These could include

● letters of enquiry
● letters giving information
● letters confirming appointments
● letters of complaint
● letters to job applicants
● letters of reminder
● circular letters
● form letters.

To create a good impression, a business letter should

● be correctly set out
● be neatly typed with no errors or messy corrections
● be courteous and polite – not abrupt or nasty
● not have any spelling, punctuation or grammatical errors.

Most business letters today are set out in fully-blocked style with open punctuation. Look at the example below.

Interior Design Company

Lakeland House, Orpington Place, Oxford OX2 3PZ TEL: 0865-473527 FAX: 0865-246678

Our ref NE/GHT
Your ref 234/RT

14 April 199

Mr Paul Hastings
Texline Products plc
41 Highbury Gardens
OXFORD
OX2 9TX

Dear Mr Hastings

REFURBISHMENT OF RECEPTION AREA

Thank you for your letter of 10 April returning fabric samples. I note your comments with regard to styles and enclose one of our design brochures for you to look at.

I have arranged for work to commence on Monday, 21 April next. It would assist our fitters if the whole of the reception area could be cleared of furniture before they arrive. The work should take three days to complete so the area should be usable by Thursday, 24 April.

If you require any further information about the work, please do not hesitate to contact me.

Yours sincerely
INTERIOR DESIGN COMPANY

WEdwards

Nigel Edwards
Manager

Points to remember

✓ Use a heading, if necessary – it can save a long explanation of what the letter is about.

```
VACANCY FOR ACCOUNTS CLERK
Patent No 73456
```

✓ Although punctuation is omitted from the date, name and address of the addressee, full stops and commas should be used in the body of the letter to assist the reader.

✓ An opening paragraph sets the scene.

We thank you for your letter …
As arranged at our meeting yesterday …

Never

I am writing this letter to tell you …
With reference to your letter of …

✓ The middle paragraph(s) should cover the reasons for writing the letter e.g. to give information, to offer an explanation, to request more detail.

✓ The last paragraph should conclude the letter in a friendly manner.

If you require any further information, please …
We look forward to hearing from you…

✓ The salutation and complimentary close should match.

Dear Sir (Madam)	use	*Yours faithfully*
Dear Mr Kinder	use	*Yours sincerely*

✓ Do not ramble on trying to make the letter longer than necessary. Some letters only need to be short!

You work for Peter Anderson, the Valuations Director of Shireburn Homes Ltd. He has asked you to prepare three letters for him to sign on his return to the office later. His written instructions for the letters are set out below.

Letter 1

Write to Mrs Susan Parkinson of the Evergreens, Valley Road, Churchtown CH5 7RD.

I spoke to her by telephone yesterday and arranged to call at her house on Friday of next week at 2.30 pm. Can you confirm this appointment?

Ask her to collect her house deeds from her bank so that I can check who owns the plot of land at the rear of her house.

Letter 2

Write to Tony Parks of Jubilee Garage, Singleton Road, Churchtown CH1 4FG. Thank him for his letter dated yesterday.

Tell him I have discussed the question of car leasing with my fellow directors and would like more information from him. Ask him to send some quotations for me to look at.

In the meantime, ask him to collect the Escort van next Thursday for a six-monthly service.

Letter 3

Write to the Manager of Lloyds Bank, High Street, Churchtown CH2 3FB, Use the heading: Account No 12736453.

Tell him I was surprised to see from my monthly statement that a direct debit for £61.75 to Mercury Finance was taken out of my account this month.

I cancelled this debit last month. Ask him to check the matter and make arrangements to reimburse my account.

Tone

A business letter is usually written more formally than a letter to a friend. Compare the differences in tone in the following excerpts.

Business letter	Letter to a friend
If you require further information do not hesitate to telephone me	Give me a ring
Thank you for your letter of yesterday	How nice to hear from you
An early reply will be appreciated	Drop me a line early next week
I suggest that we meet to discuss the matter	Let's meet so we can catch up on what's happened

Letters to friends are more chatty and often written in the same tone we would use if we were speaking to that person.

It is important when you are sending out letters for your company that you use a business-like tone.

Memos

- **Memo** is the abbreviated form for the word **memorandum**. The plural of memorandum is memoranda (not memorandums).
- A memo is used when writing to people who work in your own organisation.
- Memos do not need to show the recipient's address because they are usually going to someone in your own building.
- They should be kept short and to the point.
- If the memo is to contain a considerable amount of information, divide this into numbered points for clarity.
- A salutation and complimentary close are also unnecessary, although the sender sometimes initials the memo at the end.
- Memos dealing with a confidential matter should be marked 'Confidential'. They should be put in a sealed envelope, similarly marked.

Here are two examples of memo layout.

```
M E M O R A N D U M

From    Louise Nelson              Ref    LN/

To      Charles Kay               Date   24 January 199-


MARKETING MEETING


The date for next month's marketing meeting has had to be
changed because Mr Parker will be in Germany on that date.

The meeting has been rescheduled for 27 February at 10 am in
the Board Room.

        LN
```

```
                        MEMORANDUM

To      Jane Fairfax

From    Mike Newton

Date    12 January 199-

Ref     MN/ASD


Holiday Rota

I attach the holiday rota list for this year.

Will you please make sure that everyone in your department
enters the dates when they would like to take their holidays.

Can I remind you that where more than three people want to
take their holidays at the same time, those in the most senior
positions have first choice.

        MN

Enc
```

Your boss, Jeremy Lucas, has asked you to book a single room with private facilities for
Thursday of next week (one night – bed and breakfast only) at the Carlton Hotel, Brighton.
You have made the reservation by telephone and sent them a letter confirming the booking.

Write a **memo** to your boss confirming what you have done.

Fill in the missing letters, then write the words in your folder to help you remember them.

1 A _yph_n is used to connect two words.

2 If you are unsure about the spelling of a word, check with a __ct__n_ry

3 A ___o is a written communication to someone in your own organisation.

4 Yours faithfully is a type of c__pl_m__t_ry close.

5 The _p_st___h_ is a punctuation sign used to show ownership.

6 Reading a newspaper regularly will help to extend your __c_b_l__y.

7 Memos should, if possible, be kept ___rt.

8 A c___n is used before introducing a list.

9 Business letters are generally set out in full-blocked s_y__.

10 All written communications should be checked carefully for errors in _p_ll__g.

Wordsearch

Look at the grid shown below and find the following words.

GRAMMAR

LAYOUT

SALUTATION

CONFIRMATION

LETTER

SPELLING

DASH

ENQUIRY

SENTENCE

PUNCTUATION

C	R	W	S	P	E	L	L	I	N	G	D
S	O	D	F	V	X	X	F	Y	R	E	P
A	E	N	Q	U	I	R	Y	C	S	H	U
Q	L	V	F	B	R	Y	H	P	W	S	N
H	A	E	B	I	W	P	V	R	K	A	C
D	Y	C	B	W	R	K	Y	E	W	D	T
B	O	N	G	R	A	M	M	A	R	W	U
P	U	E	D	F	H	J	A	D	W	U	A
V	T	T	J	H	L	E	T	T	E	R	T
S	X	N	K	L	Q	S	T	P	I	W	I
D	B	E	K	R	E	T	Y	H	J	O	O
S	W	S	A	L	U	T	A	T	I	O	N

11   Applying for a job

Towards the end of your training, you will be thinking about applying for a job.

By now you will probably have formed a definite idea of the type of work you would like to do.

Generally, the larger the organisation, the more specialised the work, e.g.

copy typist
word processing operator
data processing clerk
filing clerk
receptionist.

A smaller office may offer the opportunity of more varied duties which may include all of the following:

answering the telephone
dealing with callers
handling the mail
some filing, reprography, typing or word processing.

Look for vacancies in your local newspaper, the careers office or a job centre.
Perhaps your college or training agency receives details of vacancies.

Prepare a **curriculum vitae (CV)** of your achievements. Ask your tutor to check your draft for spelling mistakes or to see if you have left anything out.

Use a word processor so that the CV can be updated, e.g. when examination results are received.

You may like to use the layout on the following page.

Do check that people are willing to let you use their name as a referee.
They could include

college tutors
present or previous employers (including a part-time job)
secondary school year head
supervisor of any voluntary work undertaken by you
a longstanding friend of the family holding a position of responsibility.

CURRICULUM VITAE

NAME:

ADDRESS:

TELEPHONE:

DATE OF BIRTH:

EDUCATION:

QUALIFICATIONS:

RESULTS AWAITED:

WORK EXPERIENCE:

REFERENCES:

INTERESTS:

A short, neat, handwritten or typed letter should accompany your C.V.

17 Temple Gardens
Bridgetown
BR2 3GK

6 May 199 -

The Manager
BKR Manufacturing Company
27–31 Taylor Street
BRIDGETOWN
BR1 7KZ

Dear Sir

I would like to be considered for the position of clerk/typist which was advertised in the Bridgetown Evening News.

My one-year secretarial course at Bridgetown College finishes at the end of the month and I enclose a copy of my CV showing what I hope to achieve.

I look forward to hearing from you in due course.

Yours faithfully

Julie Prescott

Use good quality paper (*never* a page torn from an exercise book).

Buy a pack of matching DL white envelopes and use the minimum number of folds for your letter and CV. This will create a good first impression with the person receiving your application.

Draft out your CV, using the example on the previous page. Ask your tutor to check it before preparing and printing it on a word processor.

Write out or type a letter to accompany your CV applying for the following vacancy.

RECEPTIONIST

Must have excellent telephone manner, knowledge of computers and word processing.

Hours 9 am – 5.15 pm, half hour lunch.
Wage negotiable. Please send CV to:

Ms Jackie Nixon
Groupe Panache
Daisy Hill Estate
Ashworth Street
BRIDGETOWN
BR3 6QT

12 The interview

Preparation

● Find out all you can about the organisation. Interviewers will always be impressed by candidates who have done their homework, and you will be able to ask relevant questions during the interview.

● Find out where the organisation is located and decide how you will get to the interview. Check bus or train timetables beforehand.

● The organisation may have sent you an application form to complete, prior to the interview. Take a photocopy to enable you to draft out your answers before completing the form neatly.

● Decide before the actual day what you will wear to the interview and make sure the outfit is clean and pressed. Do not leave this job until a few hours before you go!

Choose an outfit in which you feel smart and comfortable – perhaps a suit or a jacket and skirt. Avoid micro skirts and jeans.

Check that hair, nails and shoes are clean.

● Think about the possible questions you may have to answer and plan your answers *now*!

  – What subjects were included in your training course?
  – What made you apply for this position?
  – Why are you seeking new employment?
  – Tell me about yourself.

Do not leave any of these things until the morning of the interview!

On the day

● Avoid arriving late at all costs. (Remember your preparation.)

● When meeting your interviewer, shake hands firmly.

● Take a seat only when invited to do so.

● Put your case or handbag by the side of your chair (don't forget it when you leave).

● Look the interviewer in the eye when you talk.

● Avoid smoking, even if invited to do so.

● Be prepared to enlarge on your answers. Never reply just 'Yes' or 'No'.

● Remember to speak clearly and do not mumble. Avoid slang expressions and try to use correct grammar. Keep … er and … um to an absolute minimum.

- Do not mention personal details

    e.g. problems at home
            boyfriends/girlfriends.

- The interviewer will not be impressed with answers such as

    'I find my present job boring'
    'I am after more money'.

A more positive response would be

    'I enjoy my present job but I feel ready to take on more responsibility.'

- At the end of the interview, you will probably be asked if there is anything further you wish to know. You could ask

    'Will there be the possibility of day release to further my studies?'
    'What opportunities are there for promotion?'

If there is nothing you wish to ask, you could conclude the interview by saying

    'I think you have covered all aspects of the position fully and I look forward to hearing from you.'

With a colleague, practise asking and answering questions. These needn't be just work-related – any practice in speaking clearly and putting together answers is good for you. It will help you to think on your feet.

Key to Activities

1.1 Organise own work

Page 2 – reasons for unfinished work

a Absent because of sickness
Too long lunch/tea break taken
Too much time spent talking to colleagues
Work had to be repeated because of errors

b Numerous visitors had to be dealt with at reception
Given urgent jobs to do by other colleagues
Gave assistance to a colleague under pressure
Fire drill/building had to be evacuated!

c Computer breakdown/disk corrupted (no back-up copy)
Insufficient consumables to finish job e.g. photocopy paper, toner, envelopes,
letter head paper
Fault on telephone or fax lines or lines engaged
Power failure (electricity)

Page 4 – organising the workload

Suggested order of tasks
5, 7, 6, 12, 4, 13, 1, 10, 11, 3, 9, 2, 14, 8

Page 6 – section review

1 role
2 interruptions
3 priority
4 extra
5 wastage

6 on
7 1974
8 line
9 adapt
10 colleagues

Page 6 – wordsearch

1.2 Develop self to improve performance

Page 14 – section review

1 vocational
2 line manager
3 in-house
4 TEC
5 cross-reference
6 portfolio
7 appraisal
8 punctuality
9 Job Centre
10 action plan

Page 14 – wordsearch

Q	E	V	I	D	E	N	C	E	B	N	T
D	Q	Y	P	O	R	T	F	O	L	I	O
X	W	Q	A	B	N	M	Y	A	V	T	A
X	W	E	L	E	M	E	N	T	V	B	P
S	W	F	G	H	N	O	V	D	G	S	P
T	R	A	I	N	I	N	G	D	S	W	R
X	W	A	C	T	I	O	N	D	W	T	A
X	B	G	A	B	F	E	T	J	G	D	I
X	Q	C	B	O	F	E	S	W	A	J	S
V	O	N	O	F	R	T	F	L	P	D	A
V	E	R	I	F	I	E	R	F	J	M	L
B	P	F	D	C	W	C	B	G	H	J	Y

1.3 Maintain own work area to assist work flow

Page 17 – section review

1 area
2 swivel
3 important
4 suspended
5 regulations
6 telephone
7 daily
8 environment
9 repeat
10 tidy

Page 17 – wordsearch

C	D	S	W	V	B	M	Y	O	L	E	W
H	A	C	C	E	S	S	I	B	L	E	B
E	F	B	G	T	Q	A	D	B	N	K	H
C	S	W	Y	U	D	R	A	W	E	R	L
K	W	D	F	G	A	C	B	P	U	T	H
L	Q	X	W	O	R	K	F	L	O	W	Z
I	B	G	B	Q	M	A	S	D	T	T	L
S	C	Y	N	A	D	T	U	Q	W	R	B
T	E	C	E	G	J	R	W	Q	N	A	X
K	S	T	A	T	I	O	N	E	R	Y	V
A	Q	Y	P	L	W	C	V	D	E	S	K
T	T	E	L	E	P	H	O	N	E	D	B

2.1 Contribute to the preventions of hazards in the workplace

Page 18 – identifying hazards

Picture 1	Carrying too many files, fire door propped open
Picture 2	Plug socket overloaded, boiling kettle near edge of table
Picture 3	Sun glare on VDU screen, person stood on swivel chair
Picture 4	Bags lying in aisle, worn carpet
Picture 5	Waste bin being used as ashtray, person licking envelopes to seal
Picture 6	Boxes blocking emergency exit, trailing flex
Picture 7	Papers blowing onto fire, scissors on edge of desk
Picture 8	Carrying heavy equipment, filing cabinet door left open

Page 19 – additional potential hazards

- Smoking in 'no smoking' areas (particularly near flammable materials)
- Bags, articles or equipment left in passageways
- Bringing liquids (coffee, tea) into an electrical area e.g. computer room
- Boxes stacked too high
- Spillages not cleaned up immediately
- Not using correct stepladders to reach high shelves
- Running down corridors
- Not following manufacturer's instructions when using machinery
- Not following instructions when storing flammable substances

Page 24 – section review

1	HASAWA	6	legs
2	potential hazards	7	acoustic
3	machinery	8	VDU
4	temperature	9	COSHE
5	'six pack'	10	closed

Page 24 – wordsearch

Y	F	S	S	J	V	H	B	K	G	S	W
S	T	L	U	S	W	T	C	P	U	T	N
L	N	I	O	P	O	L	I	C	Y	R	Q
O	E	F	R	A	L	A	R	M	S	U	M
J	D	B	E	O	E	V	K	D	D	L	V
X	I	N	G	K	H	S	F	I	R	E	P
H	C	W	N	Y	E	T	E	G	A	S	I
N	C	H	A	U	M	C	U	O	Z	T	M
Q	A	V	D	J	M	P	J	A	A	C	T
D	F	V	F	P	Q	A	L	U	H	L	C
F	W	G	C	M	O	Q	J	L	Q	Z	M
J	L	P	E	U	X	S	A	F	E	T	Y

2.2   Contribute to the limitation of damage to persons or property in the event of an accident or emergency

Page 25 – reasons for evacuating a building

Practice fire drill   Bomb threat   Gas leak   Toxic fumes   Power failure
Flood   Risk of explosion

Page 27 – fire extinguishers

In the United Kingdom, fire extinguishers are generally colour-coded as follows:

1   red   –   water
2   blue   –   multi-purpose dry powder
3   blue   –   standard powder
4   green   –   halon
5   cream   –   AFFF (multi-purpose foam)
6   cream   –   foam
7   black   –   carbon dioxide (CO_2)

However, British Standards 5423 recommends that fire extinguishers are

● predominently colour-coded as listed above; *or*
● all predominently red with a colour-coded label; *or*
● of self-coloured metal with a colour-coded label
   (i.e. modern extinguishers are stainless steel polished).

Note: Fire extinguishers in EU countries are all predominently red, with a colour-coded label – regardless of their content.

Page 27 – suggested contents of first aid box

● individually wrapped sterile bandages
● sterile eye pads, with attachment
● sterile triangular bandages
● safety pins
● sterile unmedicated dressings (large, medium and small)
● assorted plasters
● cotton wool
● lint
● finger stall
● plastic gloves
● scissors

No drugs should be kept in first aid box!

Page 28 – completed accident report form

ACCIDENT REPORT FORM

Name of injured person *MATTHEW KINGSTON*	Age *28*

Home address
15 TENBY CLOSE
BRIDGETOWN

Department *ACCOUNTS*

Date of accident	Time *1.15 pm*

Where did accident happen? *ON STAIRS OUTSIDE CANTEEN*

How did accident occur? *SLIPPED DOWN STAIRS*

Details of injuries *BADLY GRAZED BACK AND DISLOCATED THUMB*

Details of treatment given at work *TAKEN TO FIRST AID ROOM AND ARM PUT IN SLING*

Did the injuries require hospital treatment? *YES*

Name of witness to accident *SIMON WALKER*

SIGNATURE of person reporting the accident *A. Student*

DATE *Today's date*

Page 29 – section review

1 extinguishers
2 induction
3 first aid box
4 accident book
5 blankets

6 evacuate
7 bandages
8 bomb threats
9 colour
10 safety representative

Page 29 – wordsearch

E	E	C	H	E	M	I	C	A	L	R	R
P	P	R	O	C	E	D	U	R	E	N	E
T	E	G	H	F	F	B	I	U	O	B	H
Y	O	V	W	X	G	H	W	I	V	L	S
Q	A	L	A	R	M	F	T	B	S	A	I
Y	F	P	R	C	S	C	H	E	C	N	U
R	T	Y	Y	U	U	C	G	L	P	K	G
U	S	A	N	D	W	A	L	P	T	E	N
J	W	Q	N	L	D	T	T	I	Y	T	I
N	X	I	Q	N	I	P	L	I	W	Q	T
I	S	W	A	B	R	T	M	F	O	S	X
Q	W	B	F	W	A	M	Y	O	R	N	E

2.3 Contribute to maintaining the security of the workplace and its contents

Page 30 – organisations employing security personnel

colleges
libraries
galleries
town halls
banks
airport terminals
government offices
private companies
numerous departmental stores and multiple shops
    eg Harrods
         Marks & Spencer

Page 33 – section review

1 password
2 virus
3 open
4 pen
5 photographs

6 frequently
7 identity
8 panic
9 Data Protection
10 confidential

Page 33 – crossword

			¹V	²D	U		³P		⁴D	
		⁵C		O			⁶A	L	A	R	M
	⁷B	A	D	G	E		S		T	
		M					S		A		⁸W
	⁹K	E	Y	S			W				I
		R					O				N
¹⁰U	N	A	U	T	H	O	R	I	S	E	D
S							D				O
E											W
¹¹R	E	C	E	P	T	I	O	N			S

3.1 Follow instructions and operate equipment

Page 34 – signs

1 no smoking
2 first aid
3 telephone from here
4 no turning left
5 paper jam (photocopier)

6 tourist information
7 parking permitted
8 danger – electricity
9 danger – chemical hazard
10 no entry

Page 39 – section review

Care of floppy disks

Never

1 fold disks
2 touch exposed areas
3 expose to sun/heat
4 write on disks
5 exposed to magnetic objects
6 force disks into small wallets

Always

7 store disks upright in a box
8 write the label before attaching to disk
9 take a back-up copy

Page 39 – wordsearch

Y	P	P	O	L	F	C	R	W	S	B	K
T	I	N	S	T	R	U	C	T	I	O	N
I	Z	X	W	Q	H	K	M	D	O	T	O
C	G	G	H	U	F	A	N	G	O	F	V
I	V	N	V	S	R	X	E	V	P	A	E
R	E	Q	P	G	M	D	O	P	E	U	R
T	C	X	A	B	E	M	T	Y	R	L	H
C	W	I	L	L	U	S	T	R	A	T	E
E	D	C	B	W	I	P	W	B	T	Q	A
L	G	B	V	C	F	Q	L	P	E	C	T
E	O	S	V	B	R	E	Y	U	E	W	J
G	M	A	I	N	T	E	N	A	N	C	E

Page 40 – consumables and office equipment

Listing paper –	dot matrix printer
Glass cleaner –	photocopier
Batteries –	electronic typewriter
Letter head paper –	electronic typewriter
Toner –	photocopier
Daisy wheel –	electronic typewriter
Carbon paper –	electronic typewriter
Disk box –	microcomputer
A4 bond paper –	electronic typewriter
Paper rolls –	fax machine
Photocopy paper –	photocopier
Ribbon cassettes –	electronic typewriter/dot matrix printer
Correction tapes –	electronic typewriter
OHP transparencies –	photocopier
Floppy disks –	microcomputer

Page 43 – section review

1 germs
2 soft
3 exposure
4 weak
5 labelled

6 rolls
7 daisy
8 communicating
9 toner
10 COSHH

Page 43 – crossword

4.1 Create and maintain effective working relationships with other members of staff

Page 48 – section review

1 willingly
2 deadlines
3 equal
4 communicate
5 deaf

6 colleagues
7 gossip
8 apologise
9 title
10 discriminate

Page 48 – wordsearch

H	C	O	L	L	E	A	G	U	E	Y
S	F	G	U	G	K	P	A	D	T	N
G	C	E	A	T	P	O	U	R	T	R
C	X	M	P	U	O	T	U	E	E	C
G	I	B	F	D	L	O	R	S	E	A
G	U	O	G	H	I	K	O	S	R	L
F	S	H	T	V	T	U	R	F	C	L
C	L	E	A	N	E	B	V	H	S	E
F	E	H	T	G	H	R	E	W	I	R
K	E	S	T	A	N	D	A	R	D	S
B	K	U	W	O	R	K	L	O	A	D

4.2 Greet and assist visitors

Page 50 – non-verbal communications

1 C
2 D
3 A
4 B

Page 54 – section review

1 greeting
2 delay
3 image
4 introducing
5 security

6 escort
7 difficult
8 appointments
9 confidential
10 register

Page 54 – crossword

			¹I	M	A	G	E		²B	A	G	S	
		³N							A				
⁴L	O	C	K	E	D				D			⁵S	
	N								G			E	
	V		⁶P	O	L	I	T	E				C	
	E		R									U	
	R		O		⁷V	I	S	I	T	O	R	
	B		M									I	
⁸A	P	P	O	I	N	T	M	E	N	T		
	L		T									Y	

5.1 Process incoming and outgoing telecommunications

Page 62 – incorrect messages

7 March	– no date given
8 March	– no telephone number for daughter's house
9 March	– only 3 reps' names given
10 March	– time message received is omitted
11 March	– total of £120 is incorrect, should be £110
12 March	– message too brief – not clear

Page 65 – telephone numbers and codes

1–8	no key possible
9	010 353 1
10	010 34 22
11	010 39 6
12	010 49 89

Pages 72-73 – section review

(missing words)

1 secrecy
2 standard
3 VDU
4 TouchTone
5 *Yellow Pages*
6 answering
7 message
8 extensions
9 reference
10 freefone

(missing letters)

1 extension
2 alphabet
3 day
4 question
5 urgent
6 pen, pencil
7 verbal
8 neatly
9 name
10 time

Page 73 – wordsearch

R	B	O	P	E	R	A	T	O	R	S
D	I	R	E	C	T	O	R	Y	E	Y
J	N	S	G	H	J	I	Y	G	E	C
C	T	R	H	E	J	K	A	Y	S	N
H	E	S	W	A	Z	P	X	N	T	E
A	R	D	G	P	W	F	H	G	A	G
R	N	G	T	O	E	A	W	S	N	R
G	A	L	L	P	I	U	T	E	D	E
E	L	L	A	S	X	L	C	Q	A	M
S	E	C	U	R	I	T	Y	Y	R	E
Y	S	E	Q	S	D	S	G	Y	D	T

5.2   Supply information to meet specified requests

Page 76 – where to find information

1 AA handbook, travel agent
2 Travel agent, bank, newspaper
3 Travel agent, teletext
4 *Who's Who*
5 Dictionary
6 Mileage distance chart in a diary, road atlas or AA handbook
7 Newspaper, *Radio Times* or teletext
8 Newspaper, teletext
9 Post Office Counters Ltd
10 Parcelforce

Page 78 – section review

(missing words)

1 dictionary
2 directory
3 viewdata
4 microfiche
5 colleagues
6 oral
7 index
8 deadline
9 newspaper
10 graph

(finding information)

1 subject to change
2 071
3 Solent
4 Member of the European Parliament
5 subject to change
6 subject to change
7 Valletta
8 subject to change
9 Roberts
10 *Curriculum vitae*

5.3 Check and process routine, numerical information

Page 79 – numerical errors

1 Telephone number transposed – should be 0772-614328
2 Amount transposed – should be £1097.64
3 Figures not aligned – total should be 7805
4 Decimal point was not inserted in calculator – should be £82.89
5 £2000 (not £200)
6 Incorrect subtraction – total should be 5601
7 21p should be inserted in calculator as .21 – total should be £68.46
8 10006 (zero omitted)

Page 83 – section review

1 £379.80
2 £415.84
3 £966
4 £118.26
5 £8539

6 £347.75
7 23816
8 100032; 1000600; 10004
9 £3.50
10 9 years

Page 84 – wordsearch

W	E	Y	T	G	F	F	R	T	H	B	P
E	W	R	T	I	N	V	O	I	C	E	U
Q	C	A	L	C	U	L	A	T	O	R	B
E	H	R	G	D	X	Z	A	Q	T	N	S
S	E	C	R	A	N	D	O	M	C	R	Z
O	C	S	B	W	P	T	I	B	O	W	C
P	K	A	W	V	B	A	C	R	B	N	L
S	V	L	B	N	L	N	R	C	A	Q	F
N	D	I	S	C	R	E	P	A	N	C	Y
A	R	G	B	Y	T	U	O	V	F	J	M
R	V	N	U	M	E	R	I	C	A	L	K
T	V	B	N	M	H	G	T	R	E	S	W

6.1 Store information using an established storage system

Page 86 – documents for filing

letters received
copy letters
memos
orders
quotations
delivery notes

invoices
statements
receipts
insurance documents
legal documents

Page 86 – alphabetical order

Adams, R & Co Ltd
Adamson, Paul
Black, R
Black, Robert
Bread Shop, The
Clark, Pauline
Clarke, Peter
Environment, Department of the

Green, Trevor
Greengate Hotel
McIvor, Julian
St Thomas' Nursery
Samuel, Charles
7-day Service Company
VDU Sales Ltd
Vintage Wine Company

Page 87 – numerical order

731 – P Bentley
7249 – S Belling
7543 – D Botham
7621 – L Boston
73814 – D Burgess
74256 – K Berry

74723 – A Barker
75231 – W Battersby
76241 – R Bodworth
77472 – T Barton
77571 – R Bottomly
77593 – M Bickley

Page 89 – index cards

Name	FOSTER, STEPHEN	Number	3742
Address	27 CANTERBURY WAY BRISTOL BS98 4RG		
Telephone No 0272 576684		Date of birth 27-12-55	
Details			

Name	DIXON, PAULINE	Number	2895
Address	49 PRINGLE DRIVE DUNFERMLINE KY45 9KJ		
Telephone No 0383 463532		Date of birth 12-06-71	
Details			

Name	SHAIKH, HANIF	Number	2832
Address	48 PORTLAND STREET LEICESTER LE2 7DD		
Telephone No 0533 564739		Date of birth 14-9-60	
Details			

Name	O'DRISCOLL, JOHN	Number	3275
Address	312 DEVONPORT ROAD PRESTON PR5 2FG		
Telephone No 0772 465832		Date of birth 08-08-65	
Details			

Page 91 – microfiche readers

reference libraries
banks
building societies

Pages 96–97 – section review

(identifying equipment)	*(order of missing words)*	*(missing letters)*
1 vertical cabinet	release	1 database
2 wallet folder	sorted	2 fields
3 card index box	alphabetical	3 sorted
4 file labels	numerical	4 report
5 box file	index	5 back up
6 suspension filing	vertical	6 password
7 punch	suspended	7 Data Protection
8 ring binder	cross-reference	8 heat
9 stapler	confidential	9 connections
10 filing stool	microfiche	10 overwriting

Page 98 – wordsearch

E	X	E	O	Y	U	P	T	L	W	N
B	L	K	H	M	Q	L	T	J	K	P
W	V	E	D	F	T	U	U	V	D	U
A	C	H	C	O	O	E	T	E	I	K
F	A	U	L	T	S	Z	U	P	S	C
W	Q	P	N	J	R	D	F	G	K	A
E	R	I	R	E	P	O	R	T	O	B
H	R	E	C	O	R	D	N	N	E	W
P	A	S	S	W	O	R	D	I	P	R
V	B	W	R	H	J	I	R	E	C	Q
V	L	Y	D	A	T	A	B	A	S	E

6.2 Obtain information from an established storage system

Page 99 – index card details

Full name
Address (including post code)
Date of birth
Telephone number
Reference number

Other information could include a credit limit. Personal details (such as telephone number) can be obtained from the index card, thus avoiding the need to borrow the file.

Page 100 – absent card

OUT

FILE BORROWED	BORROWER'S NAME	DEPARTMENT	DATE BORROWED	DATE RETURNED
~~CONTROL SERVICES PLC~~	~~Jane Mortimer~~	~~Accounts~~	~~3 February~~	~~5 February~~
~~HAMILTON & CO~~	~~Fatima Sidal~~	~~Purchasing~~	~~7 February~~	~~7 February~~
~~KEY BUSINESS SYSTEMS~~	~~Julie Carter~~	~~Technical~~	~~9 February~~	~~13 February~~
~~MEHMOOD KHAN~~	~~Gary Rogers~~	~~Personnel~~	~~15 February~~	~~16 February~~
STAR ENGINEERING PLC	Tony Wilkins	Sales	21 February	

Page 101 – explanation for missing file

Points to include:
- Explain immediately why file is not available.
- Use a polite, informative manner.
- Give name of the person who is currently using the file and how long the file has been absent.
- State what action you will be taking to retrieve the file.

Action to take
You *could* request the filing clerk to chase up the file from Simon Boston
or ask Simon Boston yourself if he has finished using the file
or ask if he would be prepared to let Mr Kingsley borrow the file after which you will return it to him.

Page 102 – section review

1 alignment
2 alphabetical
3 wallet, manilla
4 suspension
5 cross-reference
6 confidential
7 departmental
8 out, absent
9 reminder
10 safety

Page 102 – crossword

```
          1I                    2D
        3N U M E R I C A L            4C
          D                T           H
        5D E S K S O R T E 6R          A
      7D   X                E          S
      A           8L A T E R A L       E
      I                     E          U
      9L E G A L      10S            A  P
      Y              H              S
         11C E N T R A L I S E D
                     E
         12O V E R D U E
```

7.1 Produce text using a keyboard

Page 103 – jobs involving keyboards

secretary
typist
word processing operator
data processing operator
accounts clerk
computer programmer
travel clerk
telesales on newspapers

mail order telephonist
credit card customer services
bank clerk
building society cashier
insurance clerk
receptionist
etc.

Page 106 – identifying errors

1 committee
2 separate
3 catalogues
4 accommodation
5 occasions

week's
mail. (not?)
companies. (insert full stop)
Venice, (insert comma)
jeans? (not full stop)

Page 106 – proof-reading skills

1 Michael was looking forward to his first day at Collage has he knew the qual-ifications which he had achieved would help   him to progress atwork.

2 If most ofyour money is in a building society, A fall in intrest rates can only mean a drop on your standard of living

3 Most children watch television for atleast four hours each day? It as been sugested that this is the reason for the fall in reading standard.

4 The heaviest snowfall usually occurs in Febuary allthough heavy fall have been known to occur in march. I can remember a particularly bad year when i was a child.

Page 107 – checking by calculator

1 incorrect – should be £232.65
2 correct
3 correct
4 incorrect – balance owing is £188
5 incorrect – discount should be £37.50

Page 110 – section review

1 Correction sign's should always be marked with a different colored pen.

2 Errors could be in punctuation, spelling grammer or layout.

3 All numerical data should be checked for accuracy and any errors or omisions identified.

4 It is preferably that two people check a document - one reading and the other checking.

5 Errors should be brought to the attention of the author and amendment if neccesary.

6 The Image of the company can be spoiled by badly presented documents

7 If your spelling is poodr, you should use the spell check on your word proccessor.

8 When typing documents, always read through for error's before taking the page from your typewriter.

9 A dictionery should be used if your spelling is not to good.

10 It is sensible to use a Ruler when checking documents contain-ing figures?

Page 110 – wordsearch

7.2 Produce copies using reprographic equipment

Page 113 – photocopying costs

Company A = £185
Company B = £280
Company C = £315

Page 120 – section review

1 copyright
2 metal
3 plain
4 reprography
5 toner

6 trained
7 rental
8 scanner
9 waste
10 fastened

Page 120 – wordsearch

D	B	H	C	U	R	H	W	L	I	T	C
Z	O	F	F	S	E	T	L	I	T	H	O
U	R	G	E	N	T	P	T	N	S	E	P
B	S	T	A	P	L	E	L	E	P	R	Y
C	X	Y	K	S	T	J	N	F	G	M	R
J	M	V	T	A	D	I	P	C	N	A	I
X	K	T	L	K	L	F	R	K	I	L	G
F	D	L	D	D	C	L	O	G	D	L	H
B	O	M	A	F	L	Y	F	F	U	I	T
C	R	E	P	R	O	G	R	A	P	H	Y
K	D	U	P	L	I	C	A	T	I	N	G

8.1 Receive, sort and distribute mail

Page 123 – remittances book

REMITTANCES BOOK		DATE ....Today's date............		
Name of sender	Method of payment	Amount £ p	Account number	Signature
Calvert Bros	cheque	426 50	67245	A Student
K Higson	cash	80 00	23694	A Student
Paul Banks	cheque	73 96	32463	A Student
Anwar Hussain	cheque	32 80	34895	A Student
P O'Brien	cheque	895 00	12423	A Student
S Anderson	cash	65 00	23574	A Student
T Dickinson	postal order	5 00	43286	A Student
Cashier's signature ....*A Tutor*....................				

Page 124 – section review

1 internal	6 damage
2 confidential	7 sorted
3 knife	8 routeing
4 envelopes	9 remittances
5 urgent	10 suspicious

Page 124 – wordsearch

```
S M D R H N C J P L Q C
A E F B D Q O P V S O S
D S T H P I G E O N S E
D S B C V X Q U F B L C
E E R O U T E I N G B N
X N S Q W X D W Q B V A
L G N C M E Y P Q S J T
B E M J N C B A S K E T
B R J T N K L U I O R I
Q C I R C U L A T E B M
F A X B N P R I V A T E
L B Q R T C O U R I E R
```

8.2 Dispatch mail

Page 133 – section review

1 internal	6 registered
2 enclosures	7 jiffy
3 window	8 postage
4 envelope	9 scales
5 Parcelforce	10 cardboard

Page 133 – wordsearch

```
M A I L R O O M L D P
D R E H J F D S I E M
G V E N H G F R A A A
N W Q G H O J G M D T
I F S H I J T A R L S
K G J P F S H K I I O
N E R H J D T W A N P
A D U P L N M E F E A
R S W I F T A I R S T
F R E E P O S T T E A
S D G R E C O R D E D
```

9.1 Monitor and request stock

Page 135 – missing letters

1 A4 bond paper
2 A4 bank paper
3 letter head paper
4 carbon paper
5 card
6 labels
7 envelopes
8 message pads
9 document folders
10 pencils
11 ball point pens
12 correction fluid
13 adhesive tape
14 staplers and staples
15 scissors
16 hole punches
17 rubber stamps
18 bulldog clips
19 paper clips
20 elastic bands

Page 134 – additional consumables

memo paper
photocopy paper
envelopes – all sizes
floppy disks
folders – all types
fax rolls
felt-tip pens
pencil sharpeners
Sellotape
string
calculator batteries
graph paper
index cards
padded postage bags
disk boxes
tally rolls
daisy wheels
erasers
rubber thimbles
drawing pins
brown paper
ink stencils

Page 134 – picture identification

1 paper knife
2 box file
3 paper clip
4 bulldog clip
5 lever arch file
6 hole reinforcement stickers
7 paper punch
8 file clip
9 staple remover
10 typewriter ribbon cartridge
11 spiral-bound notepad
12 computer printout paper
13 diskette box
14 floppy disk
15 typewriter correction ribbon
16 date stamp
17 wallet folder
18 message pad

Page 136

The stock room and stationery cupboard should be kept locked to stop stealing and people helping themselves to stationery which would not be recorded on the stationery record card. The balances in stock would therefore be incorrect.

Page 137

1 Large, bulky items would be difficult to place and retrieve from top shelves.
2 Frequently requested items should be easy to reach, without the need for steps and stools – saves time.
3 If small items were unseen, assumption could be that they were out of stock.
4 Pens and pencils could roll to back or roll off shelves.
5 Old stock items should always be used first. Existing stock could deteriorate or become out of date.
6 Dampness can affect the quality of paper, it can become crinkly, therefore unsuitable for using in photocopier.

Page 137 – Georgia Kingston's approval

Georgia Kingston's approval is needed to discourage staff from ordering unnecessary stationery and to prevent pilferage.

Page 138 – stationery requisitions

STATIONERY REQUISITION

FROM *Mark Greenwood*   DATE *17 Nov 199-*

DEPT *Technical*   REQ NO   731

Please supply:

Quantity	Item
4 pkts	A4 bond paper
1 box	Staples

Signed: ....

Approved by: ....

STATIONERY REQUISITION

FROM *Sarah Longworth*   DATE *17 Nov 199-*

DEPT *Secretarial* REQ NO   732

Please supply:

Quantity	Item
5 pkts	A4 bond paper
6 bttls	correction fluid
4 reams	A4 letter head paper

Signed: ....

Approved by: ....

STATIONERY REQUISITION

FROM *Hanif Sidat*   DATE *17 Nov 199-*

DEPT *Sales*   REQ NO   733

Please supply:

Quantity	Item
8 pkts	A4 bond paper

Signed: ....

Approved by: ....

STATIONERY REQUISITION

FROM *Jennifer Thomas*   DATE *17 Nov 199-*

DEPT *Admin*   REQ NO   734

Please supply:

Quantity	Item
1 ream	A4 letter head paper
6 bttls	correction fluid
2 boxes	staples

Signed: ....

Approved by: ....

Page 139 – section review

1	requisition	6	new
2	flammable	7	bottom
3	labelled	8	ammonia
4	ladders	9	punch
5	smoke	10	bond

Page 139 – wordsearch

R	E	Q	U	I	S	I	T	I	O	N	S
E	C	G	W	N	X	Z	J	O	P	E	A
C	F	L	S	C	N	W	Q	R	L	Q	M
O	H	H	N	A	R	I	B	B	O	N	S
R	L	C	B	M	X	S	A	F	E	T	Y
D	K	N	F	L	A	M	M	A	B	L	E
S	C	U	Q	P	U	K	H	F	T	Y	A
X	B	P	K	S	C	I	S	S	O	R	S
H	V	E	N	V	E	L	O	P	E	S	B
S	Q	O	B	V	H	K	G	R	T	Y	E
O	C	S	T	A	T	I	O	N	E	R	Y
V	T	R	U	T	Q	W	H	N	B	C	P

9.2 Issue stock items on request

Page 141 – stock records

1 80 batteries should be ordered to restore maximum balance.
2 Supplier – Summit Lighting Company

Page 141 – stationery record cards

STATIONERY RECORD CARD

ITEM: ...A4 BOND PAPER... MAX: 500

SUPPLIER: STOCKTON PAPER COMPANY MIN: 50

Date	Quantity received	Quantity issued	Dept	Req No	Balance in stock
1 Nov					83
10 Nov		6	Sec	698	77
10 Nov		16	Admin	699	61
17 Nov		4	Tech	731	57
17 Nov		5	Sec	732	52
17 Nov		8	Sales	733	44

STATIONERY RECORD CARD

ITEM: ...CORRECTION FLUID... MAX: 100

SUPPLIER: OFFICE EQUIPMENT PLC MIN: 20

Date	Quantity received	Quantity issued	Dept	Req No	Balance in stock
1 Nov					65
3 Nov		3	Tech	671	62
10 Nov		6	Sec	702	56
17 Nov		6	Sec	732	50
17 Nov		6	Admin	734	44

STATIONERY RECORD CARD

ITEM: ...STAPLES... MAX: 50

SUPPLIER: OFFICE EQUIPMENT PLC MIN: 10

Date	Quantity received	Quantity issued	Dept	Req No	Balance in stock
1 Nov					18
5 Nov		5	Sec	675	13
17 Nov		1	Tech	731	12
17 Nov		2	Admin	734	10

STATIONERY RECORD CARD

ITEM: ...A4 LETTER HEAD PAPER... MAX: 300

SUPPLIER: STOCKTON PAPER COMPANY MIN: 50

Date	Quantity received	Quantity issued	Dept	Req No	Balance in stock
1 Nov					56
10 Nov		2	Sec	702	54
17 Nov		4	Sec	732	50
17 Nov		1	Admin	734	49

2 The items which need re-ordering are:

A4 bond paper

staples

A4 letter head paper

Page 142 – updating stationery record cards

STATIONERY RECORD CARD

ITEM: ...A4 BOND PAPER... MAX: 500

SUPPLIER: STOCKTON PAPER COMPANY MIN: 50

Date	Quantity received	Quantity issued	Dept	Req No	Balance in stock
1 Nov					83
10 Nov		6	Sec	698	77
10 Nov		16	Admin	699	61
17 Nov		4	Tech	731	57
17 Nov		5	Sec	732	52
17 Nov		8	Sales	733	44
29 Nov	456				500

STATIONERY RECORD CARD

ITEM: ...CORRECTION FLUID... MAX: 100

SUPPLIER: OFFICE EQUIPMENT PLC MIN: 20

Date	Quantity received	Quantity issued	Dept	Req No	Balance in stock
1 Nov					65
3 Nov		3	Tech	671	62
10 Nov		6	Sec	702	56
17 Nov		6	Sec	732	50
17 Nov		6	Admin	734	44

STATIONERY RECORD CARD

ITEM: ...STAPLES... MAX: 50

SUPPLIER: OFFICE EQUIPMENT PLC MIN: 10

Date	Quantity received	Quantity issued	Dept	Req No	Balance in stock
1 Nov					18
5 Nov		5	Sec	675	13
17 Nov		1	Tech	731	12
17 Nov		2	Admin	734	10
29 Nov	40				50

STATIONERY RECORD CARD

ITEM: ...A4 LETTERHEAD PAPER... MAX: 300

SUPPLIER: STOCKTON PAPER COMPANY MIN: 50

Date	Quantity received	Quantity issued	Dept	Req No	Balance in stock
1 Nov					56
10 Nov		2	Sec	702	54
17 Nov		4	Sec	732	50
17 Nov		1	Admin	734	49
29 Nov	251				300

Page 143 – recording where stationery goes

The stationery record cards will show to which departments the stock has been issued.

Page 144 – section review

1 requisition
2 consumable
3 hazardous and flammable
4 obsolete
5 emergency

6 legislation
7 discrepancy
8 legible and accurate
9 reconciliation
10 manual and computerised

Page 144 – wordsearch

S	D	G	H	J	E	Q	E	W	P	Y	P
S	F	O	L	D	E	R	S	V	H	C	L
C	A	R	B	O	N	D	W	C	O	N	L
W	I	A	N	S	C	Q	R	T	I	A	L
Q	N	K	L	B	O	N	D	Q	T	P	M
Z	O	M	W	A	L	L	E	T	S	E	P
C	M	A	I	P	A	P	E	R	A	R	N
M	M	D	F	G	H	F	D	T	L	C	L
Q	A	V	C	S	T	Y	K	J	E	S	M
W	W	B	U	L	L	D	O	G	X	I	C
S	W	E	Y	P	N	G	F	S	A	D	C
D	K	T	W	R	T	P	L	V	X	S	W

10   Improving your writing skills

Page 146 – grammar

1 were
2 taught
3 is

4 anywhere
5 taller
6 are

Page 149 – homonyms

1 **a** wear   **b** were   **c** where
2 **a** there   **b** their
3 **a** too   **b** two   **c** to
4 **a** has   **b** as
5 **a** fare   **b** fair
6 **a** off   **b** of
7 **a** know   **b** no
8 **a** cheque   **b** check

Page 150 – apostrophe

1 Isn't
2 you'll John's
3 There's Jack's
4 We'll manager's o'clock
5 can't it's

Page 152 – vocabulary, alternative words

1 exact, copy, same
2 double meaning, doubtful, uncertain
3 rouse, incite, annoy, cause, irritate
4 share, take part, join in
5 support, prove

Page 157 – section review

1 hyphen
2 dictionary
3 memo
4 complimentary
5 apostrophe

6 vocabulary
7 short
8 colon
9 style
10 spelling

Page 157 – wordsearch

Fire extinguishers

1 Used for class A fires
e.g. wood, cloth, paper.

Water

2 Can be used on live
electrical equipment
e.g. TV sets, computers.

Multi-purpose dry powder

3 Can also be used on live
electrical equipment.

Standard dry powder

4 Ideal for use in
car fires.

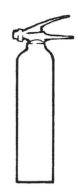

Halon 1211(BCF)

5 Can be used on class
A and class B fires
e.g. furniture fires or
paraffin heaters. More
effective than water.

*AFFF (Aqueous film-forming
foam) (multi-purpose)*

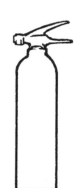

6 Used for class B fires –
a blanket of foam
smothers the flames.

Foam

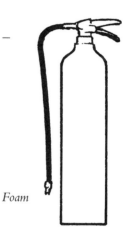

7 Clean, effective and safe
when used on live
electrical equipment.

Carbon dioxide (Co2)

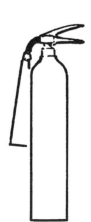

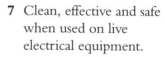

Accident report form

ACCIDENT REPORT FORM

Name of injured person	Age

Home address

Department

Date of accident	Time

Where did accident happen?

How did accident occur?

Details of injuries

Details of treatment given
at work

Did the injuries require hospital treatment?

Name of witness to accident

SIGNATURE of person reporting the accident ....

DATE ....

File

Index cards

Name	Number
Address	
Telephone No	Date of birth
Details	

Name	Number
Address	
Telephone No	Date of birth
Details	

Name	Number
Address	
Telephone No	Date of birth
Details	

Name	Number
Address	
Telephone No	Date of birth
Details	

Suggested employee record for database

EMPLOYEE RECORD

SURNAME _____ FIRST NAME _____ M/F ____

ADDRESS _____

_____

POSTCODE _____

TEL NO _____ DATE OF BIRTH _____

DEPARTMENT _____ DATE JOINED _____

STARTING SALARY _____ DATE LEFT _____

Absent card

FILE BORROWED	BORROWER'S NAME	DEPARTMENT	DATE BORROWED	DATE RETURNED

OUT

Page from a remittances book

REMITTANCES BOOK

DATE ....

Name of sender	Method of payment	Amount £	p	Signature

Cashier's signature ....

Stationery requisitions

STATIONERY REQUISITION

FROM ....   DATE ....

DEPT ....   REQ NO   731

Please supply:

Quantity	Item

Signed: ....

Approved by: ....

STATIONERY REQUISITION

FROM ....   DATE ....

DEPT ....   REQ NO   733

Please supply:

Quantity	Item

Signed: ....

Approved by: ....

STATIONERY REQUISITION

FROM ....   DATE ....

DEPT ....   REQ NO   732

Please supply:

Quantity	Item

Signed: ....

Approved by: ....

STATIONERY REQUISITION

FROM ....   DATE ....

DEPT ....   REQ NO   734

Please supply:

Quantity	Item

Signed: ....

Approved by: ....

Stationery record cards

STATIONERY RECORD CARD

ITEM: ....STAPLES.......... MAX: ..50...
SUPPLIER: ..OFFICE EQUIPMENT PLC... MIN: ..10....

Date	Quantity received	Quantity issued	Dept	Req No	Balance in stock
1 Nov					18
5 Nov		5	Sec	675	13

STATIONERY RECORD CARD

ITEM: ....A4 LETTER HEAD PAPER...... MAX: ..300.
SUPPLIER: STOCKTON PAPER COMPANY MIN: ..50....

Date	Quantity received	Quantity issued	Dept	Req No	Balance in stock
1 Nov					56
10 Nov		2	Sec	702	54

STATIONERY RECORD CARD

ITEM: ....A4 BOND PAPER......... MAX: ..500.
SUPPLIER: STOCKTON PAPER COMPANY. MIN: ..50....

Date	Quantity received	Quantity issued	Dept	Req No	Balance in stock
1 Nov					83
10 Nov		6	Sec	698	77
10 Nov		16	Admin	699	61

STATIONERY RECORD CARD

ITEM: ....CORRECTION FLUID......... MAX: ..100..
SUPPLIER: ...OFFICE EQUIPMENT PLC.... MIN: ..20....

Date	Quantity received	Quantity issued	Dept	Req No	Balance in stock
1 Nov					65
3 Nov		3	Tech	671	62
10 Nov		6	Sec	702	56

Index